DATE DUE

10-23-89/ICC	

797070

**Publication, Teaching, and the Academic
Reward Structure**

Publication, Teaching, and the Academic Reward Structure

Howard P. Tuckman
Florida State University

Lexington Books
D.C. Heath and Company
Lexington, Massachusetts
Toronto

Library of Congress Cataloging in Publication Data

Tuckman, Howard P
    Publication, teaching, and the academic reward structure.

    1. College teaching.   I. Title.
LB2331.T8   378.1'2   76-5619
ISBN 0-669-00650-5

Published simultaneously in Canada

Printed in the United States of America

International Standard Book Number: 0-669-00650-5

Library of Congress Catalog Card Number: 76-5619

To Alexander

... then in certain cases and for irresponsible men it may be that non-existent things can be described more easily and with less responsibility in words than the existent, and therefore the reverse applies for pious and scholarly historians; for nothing destroys description so much as words, and yet there is nothing more necessary than to place before the eyes of men certain things the existence of which is neither provable nor probable, but which, for this very reason, pious and scholarly men treat to a certain extent as existent in order that they may be led a step further towards their being and their becoming.

Herman Hesse

Contents

List of Tables

Preface

Several persons generously contributed their time and talents to the development of this manuscript. Alan Bayer of the Institute of Social Research at Florida State University helped the author develop the broad outline for this research, provided support under NSF-RANN grant GI-34394, and offered useful insights into the academic reward structure. His familiarity with the strengths and weaknesses of the American Council on Education surveys, as well as his healthy skepticism about the conclusions to be drawn from cross-section data, added balance to the final product. Jack Leahey and Robert Hagemann, both graduate students in the Department of Economics at Florida State University at the time the research was conducted, made valuable contributions to the programing and subsequent evaluation of the data. Mrs. Daryl Nall performed the heroic task of creating subfiles for the individual fields.

Mrs. Maryse Eymonerie of the AAUP and William Graybeals of the NEA supplied the salary data used in Chapter 1. David Breneman of the Brookings Institution and John Siegfried of Vanderbilt University offered useful suggestions incorporated in Chapter 2. Chapter 3 benefited from the comments of students in my graduate course in education policy at George Washington University and from several stimulating discussions with Jeffrey Williams and John Ortiz, then employed at the Department of Health, Education, and Welfare.

James Gapinski and Robert Hagemann spent many hours in discussion and analysis of the male-female data shown in Chapter 4. This chapter also benefited from discussions with Frank Stafford of the University of Michigan, Marianne Ferber of the University of Illinois and Maryse Eymonerie. The data in this chapter were also analyzed in a somewhat different context in papers presented at the ETS-NBER Conference at Princeton in 1975 and the American Educational Research Association Meeting in 1976.

Evaluation of the results shown in Chapter 5 was greatly aided by discussions with the following persons at Florida State University: Paul Elliot, Director of the Program in Medical Sciences; Steven Schamel, Department of Geology; Leonard Mastrogiacomo, School of Music; and Gordon Brossell, School of Education. Chapter 6 is based on the methodology developed in my article with Jack Leahey entitled "What is an Article Worth" in the October 1975 issue of the Journal of Political Economy. It reflects the many useful suggestions of John Siegfried, Jack Leahey, and George Stiegler. Chapter 7 incorporates ideas developed in a series of workshops at Florida State and in discussions with Bayer and Hagemann. I am also grateful to David Riesman for an exchange of letters which clarified my thinking on a number of points raised in both this chapter and the last one, and to Roland Liebert for sharing the fruits of his research on the grants process.

Various other people contributed to the final manuscript through their discussions with the author, including Robert Fenske, University of Arizona; Carl Lange, George Washington University; Arthur Welsh, Joint Council on Economic Education; Phillip Saunders, Indiana University; Robert Blackburn, University of Michigan; Ivan Charner, National Institute of Education; and Al Fresen and Jeff Dutton, Florida State. The responsibility for the final product is mine alone. Special thanks are due to Sheryl Horowitz for her typing assistance.

Introduction

The ends are already given—the preservation of the eternal truths, the creation of new knowledge, the improvement of service wherever truth and knowledge of high order may serve the needs of man. The ends are there; the means must ever be improved in a competitive dynamic environment.

Clark Kerr

The late sixties and early seventies saw a substantial increase in the number of books and articles exploring the world of academe. Surprisingly, the researchers in this period paid little attention to the academic reward structure and its effects on faculty behavior. It might be argued that this was because the reward structure is amorphous and unlikely to affect faculty behavior or, alternatively, that faculty are motivated by less mundane goals than other professionals. Advocates of the latter view have suggested that the fact that faculty choose a low-paying academic career provides ample proof of their lack of interest in financial rewards.

Both arguments are largely fallacious. A reward structure exists at most universities whether on a de facto or a de jure basis. It affects both who will be made financially better off and who will survive the tenure process. In part, it is shaped by the personalities that decide the rules for promotion and tenure, but it also reflects the more impersonal operation of the academic labor markets. While the value of any particular activity is not always clear in a particular department or university, the existence of a variety of institutions both demanding and supplying labor gives some semblance of rationality to the process. A faculty member ignores the realities of the academic marketplace largely at his or her own peril.

While some faculty accept a position in academe at a lower salary than they could obtain in non-academic employment, this does not mean they are uninterested in financial rewards. A decision to accept such a position implies that, for the person in question, the advantages of an academic lifestyle may have been judged to be more important than the incremental income another job would have provided. It cannot be inferred from this decision that the person's preference for an academic lifestyle is so strong that no matter how great the differential is, he or she will remain in academe. As faculty salaries fall relative to the salaries available in other pursuits, some persons will leave academe. Thus, it seems reasonable to assume that financial rewards affect faculty behavior at the margin.

The reward structure may also affect the way in which faculty allocate their time. Academic life differs considerably from that portrayed by the conventional wisdom. Beset by demands on their time, faculty choose among a large number of competing activities. The choices are often difficult and not always freely made. How many dissertations should they supervise? On which committees should they serve? How much time should be spent in grant supervision, in lecture preparation, in keeping up with the journals, in basic and applied research, and in textbook writing? At least some faculty let their choice be governed by the opportunities for reward, both financial and otherwise, that each activity offers.

The purpose of this book is to explore the nature of the reward structure at American universities. This involves an analysis of the nature of the marketplace for academic labor and an empirical investigation of the reward structure in several of the different disciplines found at the modern university.

It lies beyond the bounds of the analysis to explore all the ways that faculty derive pleasure or discomfort from the activities they perform. Interaction with students may be regenerative to some faculty and repugnant to others; department meetings may satisfy one's need for recognition or abuse one's patience; time spent in publication may be an elixir or a poison; and an administrative position may be a vehicle for creative expression or a one-way street to an ulcer. The psychic reward structure is highly complex, extremely subtle, and, however fascinating, beyond the expertise of an economist. Thus, the analysis presented below is necessarily confined to a limited number of means by which faculty behavior is rewarded.

The most direct and probably the best-known reward is the salary increment, or "merit raise," offered to faculty by their department or academic dean. A variety of such activities may be encouraged, but only a few bring a monetary reward. For example, faculty may be encouraged to develop their skill in teaching introductory courses only to learn later that self-satisfaction is the sole reward for this skill. Alternatively, a department may offer little free time for publication yet reward those who acquire this skill. It is also possible that a particular skill may be rewarded in some departments and not in others. In this instance, a reward is obtained only when, and if, a faculty member moves to a department that values that skill.

To the extent that a direct reward is given to a faculty member in the form of a yearly salary increment, its lifetime value is significantly greater than would appear if the faculty member considered only the year in which it is received. For example, a merit increment of $50 given to a young assistant professor may be reflected in his or her salary throughout that person's career. To calculate its true value, a researcher may find it useful to employ an investment framework and to discount the salary increment over the faculty member's working lifetime. Surprisingly, many students of the academic salary structure have failed to recognize this.

The direct nonmonetary satisfactions brought about by the successful exercise of a skill provide a second form of remuneration. These include the accolades of students and peers, national acclaim, and feelings of self-satisfaction and self-worth. Some evidence exists that returns of this type cumulate with time, but the efforts to quantify them have been limited.

To the extent that a faculty member's activities affect his or her chances for promotion, a third type of reward exists. Promotion usually brings a higher salary; thus it has a monetary equivalent. The resulting psychic rewards remain to be quantified, but they are likely to be considerable, at least for those who acquire tenure at the same time.

The academic reward structure has a fourth dimension: the career options, both internal and external, that result from successful exercise of a skill. Internal options take the form of access to departmental positions such as the chairmanship of a department or to universitywide offices such as a deanship or academic vice-presidency. External options include access to research grants, outside consulting, positions on national panels, opportunities to move into and out of positions in government and industry, etc. In some fields, the likelihood of exercising these options is fairly great; in others, it is virtually nonexistent. Insofar as these options emerge as a consequence of a faculty member's activities, they represent a component of the academic reward structure.

The chapters that follow develop both a conceptual and an empirical perspective on the academic reward structure. Chapter 1 sets the stage by providing information on how some of the major factors which affect the academic reward structure have changed in the recent past. A review of the literature on the determinants of academic salaries is then offered in Chapter 2. Chapter 3 presents a conceptual model of the interrelationship between the salary determination process and the academic reward structure. In Chapter 4, we address the first of several issues which arise as a result of the functioning of the reward structure, namely, whether existing efforts to overcome the past effects of discrimination against females are appropriate. Chapter 5 explores the issues raised by the creation of a single salary structure for all faculty. Chapter 6 examines the returns to publication and their implications for faculty behavior. Chapter 7 examines the allocation of faculty time, while Chapter 8 presents the conclusions of our study and their implications for the future of academe.

It is the author's hope that the materials presented in this book will contribute toward a better understanding of the academic reward structure and toward a more rational discussion of both its strengths and its weaknesses. No single effort can identify the diversity of activities that characterize the reward structures of the many individual fields. At best, it is possible to suggest that rewards affect behavior and to encourage those who are a part of the reward structure to make their criteria more explicit.

Publication, Teaching, and the Academic Reward Structure

1

The Academic Setting

The nation's fund of high-level intellectual capital on which it is now so dependent, is far from being a permanent asset. Once acquired, it wastes rapidly if its replenishment is neglected. This replenishment consists not only of support for the great libraries and museums, the research that goes on in them, and the identification and training of particularly talented students. It also consists of maintaining and strengthening the academic community's capacity to train the millions of managers, professionals and technicians who are needed in a complementary role if the nation is to make effective use of its high level intellectual capital. We owe it to future generations never to let this precious fund and the wider structure that must undergird it atrophy and deteriorate.

Alan Pifer

A growing number of students entered institutions of higher education during the sixties and early seventies. According to the Department of Health, Education, and Welfare, the number of bachelors and first professional degrees rose from 392,000 in the 1959-60 academic year to 1,005,000 in the 1972-73 academic year. During the same period, the number of masters degrees conferred rose from 74,000 to 256,000.[1]

To meet this dramatic increase in demand, existing institutions of higher education expanded, new institutions sprang up, and new branch campuses opened. Between 1959-60 and 1972-73, the number of colleges, universities, and professional schools listed in the *Education Directory* increased from 2,004 to 2,665. The net increase of 661 institutions was based on a growth of 382 two-year institutions and of 279 four-year colleges and universities.[2]

These events had serious consequences for academic labor markets. In the bright days of the sixties, graduate students could pursue their studies secure in the knowledge that a number of job opportunities awaited them after graduation. Similarly, job offers abounded for many faculty members. The salaries of the eminent rose to levels competitive with those of mid-level industry executives as many universities sought faculty to teach the growing number of new students. HEW estimates that the total number of faculty employed at institutions of higher education rose from 381,000 in the 1959-60 academic year to 825,000 in the 1969-70 academic year; an increase of 217%.[3]

1

Developments in the late sixties and early seventies severely altered the out-look for higher education. Public disenchantment with education, decreased state and Federal appropriations, forecasts of substantially diminished enroll-ments, and rising costs cast a gloomy shadow over the seventies. Some colleges reduced their offerings, others limited their enrollments, still others closed down.

The Decline in the Production of New PhDs

Between fiscal year 1966 and 1970, the number of new doctorates granted each year grew from 17,953 to 29,475, an increase of 164%. After 1970, the growth diminished. The number of new doctorates was 33,000 in 1974, a decrease of 2.2% from 1973 and about equal to the number granted in 1972. Interestingly, although the number of doctorates granted to men declined after 1972, the number received by women continued to increase.[4]

Statistics on the number of doctorate recipients are of interest for several reasons. Graduate education is labor intensive. Student-faculty ratios generally tend to be smaller at this level than at the undergraduate level, and at least some state universities provide a larger per-student subsidy to institutions engaged in graduate training. A shrinkage in the number of doctorates, to the extent that it reflects lower graduate enrollments, may mean a lower funding base and eventually a decreased demand for new faculty.

New PhDs are also an important component of the supply of educated manpower employed by institutions of higher education (IHEs). A reduction in this supply means that fewer people will be available to IHEs in the future. How this will affect academic salaries depends on what is happening to the demand for the educational services offered by IHEs.

These statistics can also be used to examine the extent to which the supply of new PhDs is responsive to starting salaries in academe. Since the production of new doctorates requires time (often in excess of four years), a reduction in starting salaries may be reflected in a reduction in the supply of new PhDs, given a suitable adjustment lag and appropriate controls for other factors.

Finally, statistics on new doctorates are important because they suggest different behavioral patterns for males and females. Figure 1-1 shows the num-ber of new doctorate recipients by fiscal year, sex, and field. As might be expected, the number of female recipients is smaller than the number of males. A large proportion of the female doctorates is concentrated in three fields, education, the social sciences, and arts and humanities, and the number of new doctorates in these fields has been increasing.

Education and the social science fields are also popular among male graduates, but the number of male doctorates in education has been falling in the seventies. Physical science docotrates constituted the largest percentage of

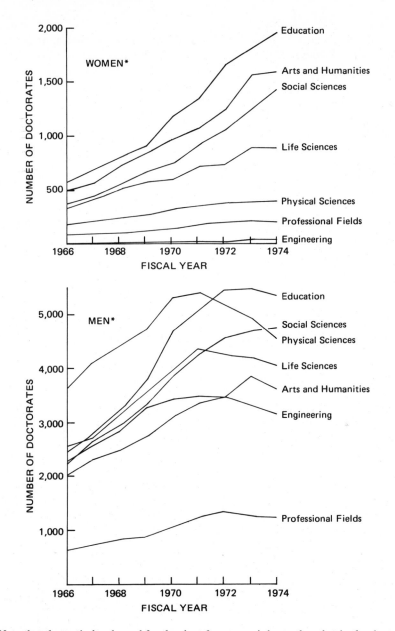

*Note that the vertical scale used for the chart for women is larger than that in the chart for men.

Source: 1974 *Summary Report of Doctorate Recipients from United States Universities*, National Research Council, Washington, D. C.

Figure 1-1. Number of New United States Doctorates by Major Field, 1966-1974

the total until 1971, but the number of new doctorates plummeted after this date. Similar declines have occurred in the life sciences and engineering, in part reflecting shifts in Federal funding away from these areas.

In contrast, the number of female doctorate recipients in these two fields has remained fairly stable. It may be that the skills or attitudes of female doctorate recipients are different than those of males; thus the determinants of labor supply may differ. Alternatively, separate labor markets may exist for the two sexes due to employer discrimination against females or other demand-related phenomena.

Federal Funds

During the early and mid-sixties, Federal payments to IHEs increased. This was partially due to the channeling of large amounts of research and development funds to the universities; it also reflected an increase in various grant and subsidy programs to students. Most Federal R&D funds were directed at a comparatively small number of prestige universities and colleges. But the effects of these funds were felt throughout academe as institutions favored by Federal funds bid research faculty away from other institutions and as Federal subsidies increased the demand for graduate training. Especially strong was the influence of Federal funds in the physical and biomedical fields and in engineering. In contrast, the social sciences received less than 5% of the research expenditures while the arts and humanities obtained virtually no funds until the National Foundation on the Arts and Humanities was created in 1965.

Statistics available from the National Science Foundation show that Federal obligations to universities (an accounting term referring to amounts available to the agencies in a given year but not necessarily spent) were about $1.4 billion in fiscal year 1963.[5] The figure rose by 14.9% in 1964, 41.9% in 1965, and 30.5% in 1966. These years correspond to what some people call the so-called golden period of higher education. In fiscal year 1967, the rate of increase was 10%, while it fell to about 2% in both 1968 and 1969. Obligations declined by 6.6% in 1970 and rose again in 1971 and 1972 by 8.1% and 18.5% respectively. They declined again in 1973 by 7.5%. The largesse of the 1960s gave way to an uneven but downward trend of Federal funding in the 1970s.

These reductions are perhaps better understood by examining their relation to the income of educational institutions. In the 1959-60 academic year, Federal funds for research and related purposes constituted 22% of the educational and general fund (E & GF) revenue reported in *Financial Statistics of Higher Education.*[6] Student aid income, largely from Federal programs, constituted another 2%. By the 1963-64 academic year, R&D and other-purpose funds rose to 27% of E&GF revenue while student aid funds remained at the 2% level.

In the 1967-68 academic year R&D funds fell to 24% of E&GF revenue while student aid rose to 3.6%. The fall in R&D continued throughout the period that followed, and by the 1972-73 academic year Federal funds for research and other purposes had shrunk to 15% of E&GF revenue while student aid income hovered at the 3.6% level.

The declines in Federal funding were made up largely by increases in student fees and state aid. Earnings from endowments fell as a percentage of educational income throughout the period; from 4.4% at the beginning of the period to 2.3% at the end. Private gifts and grants remained fairly stable at about 6% from 1959 to 1973.[7] In contrast, both student tuitions and fees and state appropriations became an increasingly large proportion of total income.

As a result of the shift in financing sources, the priorities given to particular fields and to the various activities performed by faculty appear to have shifted. We have seen in Figure 1-1 that a shrinkage occurred in the number of doctorates in the physical and biomedical sciences, fields where large doses of Federal funding were followed by severe cutbacks. It is also likely that a substantial reduction in the demand for research-oriented faculty occurred, although the data are not available to document this. In fiscal year 1967, National Research Council (NRC) data indicated that about 26% of all new PhDs planned to engage in R&D work after receiving their degrees. Another 42% planned to teach. By fiscal year 1974, the percentage planning to engage in R&D had fallen to 22% while the percentage planning to teach rose to 51%.[8]

Postgraduate Career Plans of New Doctorate Recipients

At about the same time that the expectation of falling enrollments was growing and outside funds were falling in relative terms, recipients of new doctorates began to report changes in their postgraduate career plans. Table 1-1 presents evidence of this from the NRC's study of the postgraduate plans of doctorate recipients in the U.S. in fiscal years 1970 and 1974. Data are not available prior to 1970 or on a calendar-year basis.[9] The figures indicate that a smaller percentage of doctorate recipients planned to enter educational institutions in 1974 than in 1970. However, these institutions remained the major employer of new PhDs.

The changes between 1970 and 1974 differ across the academic disciplines, suggesting that the labor-market conditions facing new doctorates differed. In 1970, 69.2% of the doctorates in mathematics planned to enter an academic institution. The comparable figures were 88.2% for those in English and American language and literature, 83.5% in history, 70.1% in political science, 52.2% in psychology, 38.9% in earth sciences, and 24.2% in physics and astronomy. In 1974, the percentages dropped to 61.4% in mathematics, 77% in English and American language and literature, 68.4% in history, 61.4% in political science,

Table 1-1
Postgraduate Career Plans of Doctorate Recipients at American
Universities, Fiscal Years 1970 and 1974

	Planning	
Planned Employment	1970	1974
Educational Institutions	56.1%	51.6%
Industry and Business	11.7	9.8
Government	7.2	8.9
Nonprofit	2.8	3.3
Other	2.5	4.0
Postdoctoral Study	14.5	14.9
Postdoctoral Status Unknown	4.9	7.5

Source: 1970 and 1974 *Summary Reports of Doctorate Recipients from United
States Universities*, National Research Council, Washington, D. C.

43.4% in psychology, 31.3% in the earth sciences, and 16.1% in physics and
astronomy. As can be seen from these figures, some fields, such as history, have
experienced relatively large reductions in the percentage of new doctorate recipients entering the market while others, such as political science, experienced
somewhat smaller reductions. In part, these differences reflect changes in the
demand for the courses in each field, but they also reflect changes in relative
supply, opportunities for employment outside academe, and a host of other
factors which have not been explored by social scientists.

Academic Salaries in the Recent Past

Having examined several of the variables affecting the market for faculty services,
we shall find it useful also to consider what happened to faculty salaries during
the same period. An analysis of the linkage between the two markets will then
be considered in the following two chapters. Unfortunately, no single historical
series on faculty salaries exists that is both representative of the broad universe of
institutions of higher education and reasonably consistent through time. The
American Association of University Professors (AAUP) publishes two series. One
provides time-series data on a limited but fixed set of schools; the other is based
on a more representative set of schools but its coverage varies through time. The
National Education Association (NEA) compiles a data series which, like the
second AAUP series, fluctuates in size from one year to the next. The National
Center for Educational Statistics also compiles a set of salary statistics with a
reporting base which fluctuates from one year to the next, and this series does
not extend back to the early years of our inquiry.

Table 1-2 presents the NEA salary data for the academic years 1957-58 to 1973-74. The figures are median salaries for faculty at each rank and for all ranks combined. Table 1-3 shows the AAUP data for the same period, also broken down by rank. The figures in the latter table, based on means rather than medians, are higher at each rank. The two series also differ in what they suggest about the biennial growth in salaries and the differentials across ranks.

The "percent change" columns in each table show the average yearly change in salary from one biennial survey to the next. These are computed by taking the percentage change for the two-year period and dividing it in half. Average and compound rates of growth are shown at the bottom of each column in each table. The average rate shows the simple percentage change from 1959 to 1969 while the compound rate shows the average annual rate of change after allowing for the increase in the salary base through time. The compound rate gives a more accurate indication of what happens biennially than does the simple average.

A roughly similar compound annual rate of growth is observed in both series over the 1959-69 period. The compound rate for the NEA all-ranks series is 5.8%; for the AAUP series, it is 5.6%. However, the similar growth rates over the long haul should not be allowed to obscure the divergence in the two series in the shorter periods. When the yearly growth rates from the two sources are correlated, the zero order correlation statistic is only 0.4. Thus, the two series suggests a somewhat different biennial pattern of growth in faculty salaries.

Differences between the series also emerge when the data are compared by rank. The NEA series shows the median salaries of associate and assistant professors falling relative to those of full professors in every year from 1957-58 to 1973-74. The NEA median salaries of lecturers and instructors and the all-ranks median fall until 1971-72 and rise thereafter. In the AAUP data for assistants, lecturers, and instructors, and the all-ranks average, a rise occurs relative to the average salary of full professors beginning in the 1967-68 academic year. However, the AAUP data indicate that the average salaries of associate professors fall relative to those of full professors until the 1971-72 academic year and rise thereafter.

While it would be desirable to select one of the above measures for comparative purposes this is not possible. Although the AAUP data are preferable for their consistency, it is not clear that they represent the broader population of higher-education institutions. The thirty-six schools in the AAUP sample are relatively well-known and with rare exceptions are prestige institutions. Most are older and established and none is predominately black or primarily oriented toward religious education. The NEA data, although presented in median form and thus less sensitive to changes in the number of institutions reporting each year, are nonetheless affected by reporting changes. Since neither series is clearly preferable, both will be used in the comparisons that follow. The choice of series is based on whether the comparison is to mean or median data.

Table 1-2
NEA Data on Median Salaries for Four-Year Colleges and Universities by Year and Rank

Academic Year	All Ranks		Full Professors		Associate Professors		Assistant Professors		Lecturers and Instructors	
	Median salary	Percent change	Median salary	Percent change	Median salary	Percent change	Median salary	Percent change	Median salary	Percent change
1957-1958	$ 6,015	---	$ 8,072	---	$ 6,563	---	$ 5,595	---	$ 4,562	---
1959-1960	6,711	5.8%	9,107	6.4%	7,332	5.9%	6,231	5.7%	5,095	5.9%
1961-1962	7,486	5.8	10,256	6.3	8,167	5.7	6,900	5.4	5,582	4.8
1963-1964	8,163	4.5	11,312	5.1	8,969	4.9	7,539	4.6	6,114	4.8
1965-1966	9,081	5.6	12,953	7.3	10,058	6.1	8,417	5.8	6,761	5.3
1967-1968	10,235	6.4	14,713	6.8	11,393	6.7	9,472	6.3	7,496	5.4
1969-1970[a]	11,745	7.4	16,799	7.1	12,985	7.0	10,698	6.5	8,416	6.2
1971-1972	12,932	5.1	18,091	3.8	13,958	3.8	11,511	3.8	9,347	5.5
1973-1974[a]	14,373	5.6	19,897	5.0	15,331	4.9	12,644	4.9	10,211	4.6
Average Rate of Growth, 1959-69	---	7.5%	---	8.4%	---	7.7%	---	7.2%	---	6.5%
Compound Growth Rate, 1959-69	---	5.8%	---	6.3%	---	5.9%	---	5.6%	---	5.1%

[a]Note that the "All Ranks" increase for this year exceeds the sum of the increases for each of the component parts.

Source: National Education Association, *Salaries Paid and Salary Related Practices in Higher Education, 1971-72*, Research Report 1972-R-5, pp. 9-11. Data for 1973-74 from Dr. William Grzybeals. Data for years before 1961 from *Salaries Paid and Salary Practices in Universities, Colleges and Junior Colleges, 1957-58 and 1959-60*.

Table 1-3
AAUP Average Salary Data for 36 Institutions by Year and Rank

Academic Year	All Ranks		Full Professors		Associate Professors		Assistant Professors		Instructors	
	Salary	Percent change	Salary	Percent change	Salary	Percent change	Salary	Percent change	Salary	Percent change
1957-1958	$ 7,760	---	$10,550	---	$ 7,700	---	$ 6,110	---	$ 4,890	---
1959-1960	8,660	5.8%	11,800	5.9%	8,530	5.4%	6,790	5.6%	5,200	3.1%
1961-1962	9,680	5.9	13,050	5.3	9,280	4.4	7,400	4.5	5,940	7.1
1963-1964	10,650	5.0	14,450	5.4	10,220	5.0	8,130	5.0	6,370	3.6
1965-1966	11,840	5.6	16,110	5.7	11,310	5.3	8,990	5.3	7,110	5.8
1967-1968[a]	13,320	6.3	17,910	5.6	12,580	5.6	10,010	5.7	7,920	5.7
1969-1970[a]	14,980	6.2	19,930	5.7	13,920	5.3	11,170	5.8	8,560	4.0
1971-1972	16,280	4.3	21,080	2.9	14,740	2.9	11,970	3.6	9,750	7.0
1973-1974	17,810	4.7	23,010	4.6	16,230	5.0	13,220	5.2	10,810	6.5
Average Rate of Growth 1959-69		7.3%		6.9%		6.3%		7.6%		8.8%
Compound Growth Rate 1959-69		5.6%		5.4%		5.0%		5.8%		6.5%

[a]Note that the "All Ranks" increase for this year exceeds the sum of the increases for each of the component parts.

Source: The figures for the period 1957-1974 were provided to the author by Mrs. Maryse Eymonerie of the AAUP staff. The sample includes: Amherst Coll., Brown Univ., Columbia Univ., Cornell Univ., Bowdoin Coll., Swarthmore Coll., Wesleyan Univ., Dartmouth Coll., Johns Hopkins Univ., Princeton Univ., Univ. of Rochester, Yale Univ., Bryn Mawr Coll., Vassar Coll., Carleton Coll., Mills Coll., Pomona Coll., Reed Coll., Wabash Coll., Oberlin Coll., Northwestern Univ., Stanford Univ., Washington Univ., Duke Univ., Emory Univ., Rice Univ., Vanderbilt Univ., California Institute of Technology, Case Institute of Technology, M.I.T., Universities of California, Illinois, Michigan, Minnesota, Washington, and Wisconsin.

Faculty Salaries after Price Adjustment

Taken in total, the figures for the 1959-74 period suggest an average annual
salary increase for faculty in the neighborhood of 5.7% a year. Even during the
so-called golden years, dramatic yearly changes in nominal income did not take
place. These statistics do not give a complete picture of how faculty fared,
however. During the late fifties and mid-sixties, the rate of inflation was fairly
low, averaging less than 1.5%[10] At the same time, real average faculty salaries
grew by somewhat over 4% a year.

By late 1965 the inflation rate had increased to 2.9% and it continued to
rise, reaching 5.9% in 1970. In real terms, average faculty salaries grew at a rate
of only about 2% from 1965 to 1970. A slight reduction in the rate of inflation
occurred in 1971, but by 1972 it had reached 6.2%. The rise did not abate in
1973, and by the end of 1974 the inflation rate exceeded 11%. During this
period, most faculty experienced a loss of purchasing power as their real incomes
fell.

Faculty Salaries and the Salaries of Other Educators

It is sometimes the case that nominal wages and salaries do not fall when the
demand for a particular type of labor decreases. However, the real salaries of
those offering labor for which the demand has diminished fail to rise at the same
rate as they do for those whose labor is in greater demand. Examination of the
relative salaries of faculty provides a way of examining how the decline in the
demand for educational services discussed earlier in this chapter has affected the
financial position of faculty.

In the sections that follow, the growth in faculty salaries is compared to the
growth in the salaries of those in other occupations. To facilitate the analysis,
the data are presented in ratio form; that is, the salary for a particular group is
shown as a percentage of the all-rank and full-professor salaries shown earlier. A
digression on the meaning of these ratios is useful. If the salary (either median or
average) of a particular profession is representative of the productivity of its
members, then the ratio of that salary to the salary of faculty may be taken to
represent the relative productivity of the two groups given several plausible
assumptions. This follows from micro economic theory, and it invites the interpretation that a rise in the ratio signifies a fall in the relative productivity of
faculty.

The difficulty with this interpretation is that it presupposes faculty are paid
their marginal product, an assumption difficult to support if academic labor
markets are imperfect. With imperfect markets, changes in the ratio may be due
to changes in relative bargaining power, movements toward or away from competitive market equilibrium, or other factors unrelated to productivity. To avoid

choosing among these alternatives at this point, no theoretical interpretation is attached to the ratios that follow. Instead, a ratio is employed strictly because of the analytic convenience it provides. When the ratio for a particular occupational group falls, this is taken to indicate that faculty salaries are rising relative to the median (or average) salary for that occupational group; when the ratio rises, it means that faculty salaries are falling behind.

We begin with an analysis of the median salaries of select college administrators. The ratios of these salaries to those of all faculty and of full professors is shown in Table 1-4. In each of the five categories, the all-ranks median salary is less than the median salary of administrators, as shown by the ratios in excess of 1. Throughout the sixties, the median salary of college presidents rose relative to the all-ranks median; no clear trend appears in the seventies.

Faculty salaries rose relative to those of the other four groups. Relative to the salaries of academic vice-presidents and provosts, the ratio first rose then fell to very close to its 1957-58 level; relative to the median salary of the deans of men and head football coaches the gain was somewhat greater. The ratio of the dean of medicine's salary to the all-faculty salary fell until the 1973-74 academic year and rose thereafter. If full professor salaries are used in the denominator for comparative purposes, the ratios become smaller but the time patterns observed above remain largely unaltered.

In all years, the median college administrator earns more than the all-faculty median salary. And, as might be expected, college presidents, academic vice-presidents, and provosts and deans of medicine have higher median salaries than those of full professors. The figures suggest that faculty have made some gains relative to administrators during the 1960s and 1970s.

In interpreting these findings, an important caveat should be borne in mind. Faculty may earn outside income from royalties, consulting, etc. Likewise, college presidents, vice-presidents and provosts and head football coaches may receive in-kind income such as free housing, household help, etc. These outside sources of income are not included in the figures presented here. Because of an absence of historical data on this type of income, the nature of the bias which this omission creates is unknown.

Faculty Salaries and the Salaries of E&S Teachers

It seems reasonable to examine the salaries of other professionals engaged in teaching in analyzing how faculty salaries fared relative to those of other occupational groups. Data are not available on the salaries of teachers in some private schools, but the NEA does collect data for elementary and secondary school (E&S) teachers.[11] The salaries of E&S teachers have traditionally been lower, presumably to reflect both the larger manpower pool available to teach school at these educational levels and a return for the extra skills required in college teaching.

Table 1-4
Median Salaries of Select College Administrators as a Proportion of the Salaries of All Faculty and Full Professors

Academic Year	College President		Academic VP or Provost		Dean of Men		Head Football Coach		Dean of Medicine	
	All	Full	All	Full	All	Full	All	Full	All	Full
1957-58	2.07	1.54	2.00	1.49	1.11	0.82	1.18	0.88	3.20	2.38
1959-60	2.06	1.52	2.11	1.55	1.08	0.86	1.19	0.86	3.03	2.24
1961-62	2.05	1.50	2.20	1.56	1.10	0.80	1.14	0.83	3.04	2.22
1963-64	2.12	1.53	2.10	1.51	1.12	0.81	1.14	0.82	3.09	2.23
1965-66	2.16	1.52	2.09	1.47	1.08	0.76	1.03	0.72	3.06	2.15
1967-68	2.18	1.52	2.09	1.45	1.07	0.75	1.02	0.71	2.96	2.06
1969-70	2.21	1.55	2.08	1.45	1.05	0.73	1.14	0.80	2.71	1.89
1971-72	2.30	1.64	1.99	1.42	1.04	0.75	1.13	0.81	2.58	1.84
1973-74	2.18	1.57	1.99	1.44	1.01	0.73	1.12	0.81	3.01	2.18

Source: Various research reports of the National Education Association from 1957 to the present. Note that these are median academic year salaries net of other forms of compensation. The "All" column shows the ratio of the median salary of administrators in a given category to the median salary of faculty in all ranks. The "Full" category gives the ratio with the median salary of full professors in the denominator.

In the 1961-62 academic year, the ratio of the median salary of elementary school teachers to the median all-ranks salary was 0.55; the comparable ratio for full professors was 0.41. By 1965-66 the respective ratios fell to 0.53 and 0.39, suggesting a relative gain for those in higher education. Thereafter, the ratios rose to 0.59 and 0.46 respectively. After 1966, the salaries of faculty fell continuously relative to those of elementary school teachers.

A similar conclusion is reached if the ratios are computed using secondary school teacher salaries in the numerator. In the 1961-62 academic year, the all-rank and full professor ratios were 0.60 and 0.44 respectively. The ratios fell to 0.57 and 0.42 in the 1965-66 academic year then rose monotonically, reaching levels of 0.62 and 0.48 respectively by 1973-74. In relative terms, college faculty were worse off at the end of the decade than at the beginning and this continued to be true in the early 1970s.

It may be argued that comparisons of this type are not relevant. E&S teacher salaries may be determined by factors quite different from those that affect college faculty. Unionization is quite strong at the E&S levels yet very weak in IHEs. Public politics and private bargaining power often play a major role in determining salaries at these levels, while faculty salaries may be less subject to these influences. The salaries of E&S teachers may be more sensitive to changes in public revenues than those of higher education faculty since a preponderant majority of the former are employed in public institutions.

Some critics may maintain that, given the current situation in the schools, E&S salaries may contain a "hazardous duty" component not found in college professors' salaries. Nonetheless, both occupational groups are primarily engaged in teaching, and some cross-elasticity of substitution is likely to exist between them.[12] The falling relative salary of those in higher education implies that, from the point of view of future teachers, E&S teaching has become somewhat more desirable from a financial point of view than it has been in the past.

Faculty Salaries and the Salaries of Other Professional Workers

In recent years, the Congress has attempted to establish comparability between the salaries of Federal civil servants and the salaries of those with similar skills in the private sector. Academic institutions have not developed a similar rule for salary determination although they may eventually move in this direction. Faculty members are among the most highly educated members of society and their skills are at least partially interchangable with those of other professionals. Thus, it seems reasonable to examine how faculty salaries have fared relative both to the salaries of professionals in the private sector and to the salaries of those in the Federal government with similar skills.

The Bureau of Labor Statistics of the U.S. Department of Labor prepares yearly data on the mean salary levels of those in the professions.[13] The BLS

surveys are broken down according to skill level, and data for a complete occupational category such as accountant or attorney are not available. The categories
are given as Accountant I, Accountant II, etc., depending on the skills a given
job requires. Wherever possible, the highest skill classification for a given class
is selected. The categories Accountant V, Auditor IV, Attorney VI, Chemist VIII,
Engineer VIII, and Director of Personnel IV are used in the comparisons which
follow. A more detailed description of these may be found in the BLS publication cited in note 13. Since the BLS uses salary averages, AAUP figures converted
to a calendar year basis are used in the comparison that follows. As a result, the
years shown in Table 1-5 differ from those presented earlier in this chapter.

Ignoring the occasional exceptions in the data, we observe a fairly consistent
pattern of declining faculty salaries. In terms of the salaries of auditors and
attorneys, faculty begin to lose in relative position after 1967. This is also true
of the figures relating accountants' salaries to those of full professors. Faculty
salaries fall relative to the average salaries of directors of personnel after 1965
(with the exception of 1969) and full professor salaries fall relative to chemists'
salaries beginning in 1967. After 1972, faculty salaries fall relative to the salaries
of all of the other professionals in the table. This accords with the patterns
found earlier, and it suggests that faculty may fall lower in the income distribution in the next few years.

Our last comparison of faculty salaries is to the salaries of Federal government employees with educational and job credentials similar to those of persons
in academe. The GS-12 civil service classification is used in the first comparison
since this is the rank at which most new PhDs enter government. Implicit in the
use of these figures is the assumption that PhDs remain in this rank throughout
their careers.

In calendar year 1961, the ratio of the average salary of GS-12s to the all-
faculty average was 1.02. The ratio fell to 0.96 in 1962 and hovered in the 0.96
range until 1966, falling to 0.94 and 0.95 in 1967 and 1968. In 1969, it climbed
back to 0.98 and in 1970 to 1.01. From 1971 on, it began to climb, exceeding
1.06 in 1974.

A similar conclusion is reached using the GS-15 average salary as a basis for
comparison to the salary of full professors. Again the choice is conditioned on
the grounds that the skills for the two types of positions are comparable. Using
this measure, we find that the ratio of government salaries to those of full
professors was 1.14 in 1960, fell to about 1.08 in the next two years, then
hovered in the 1.14 range until 1968 when it began to rise. By 1974 the ratio
was about 1.35, again suggesting a relative fall in faculty salaries. A case might
also be made for the use of the salary figure for GS-14s, but ratios calculated
with these figures suggest essentially the same conclusion.

The Current Decline in Faculty Salaries

When the results presented in the previous sections are combined, they suggest a

Table 1-5
Comparison of Faculty Salaries with those of Other Professionals

Calendar Year	Accountant V to		Auditor IV to		Attorney VI to		Chemist VIII to		Engineer VIII to		Director of Personnel IV to	
	All	Full	All	Full	All	Full	All	Full	All	Full	All	Full
1961	0.885	0.836	1.015	0.751	1.642	1.214	1.957	1.447	2.041	1.509	1.556	1.151
1963	0.919	0.803	0.977	0.722	1.695	1.251	1.920	1.418	1.936	1.430	1.525	1.126
1965	1.044	0.768	0.938	0.690	1.753	1.288	1.943	1.428	1.846	1.357	1.483	1.090
1967	0.997	0.739	0.907	0.672	1.669	1.237	1.923	1.425	1.733	1.284	1.496	1.109
1969	0.996	0.747	0.910	0.682	2.039	1.528	1.877	1.407	1.665	1.248	1.427	1.069
1971	1.050	0.800	0.956	0.728	2.107	1.606	1.876	1.430	1.688	1.286	1.507	1.149
1973	1.064	0.823	0.964	0.745	2.142	1.657	1.856	1.435	1.705	1.319	1.538	1.190

Source: Faculty data from Table 1-3 after conversion to calendar year base. Data for professional fields from U.S. Bureau of Labor Statistics, *Handbook of Labor Statistics, 1974*, Bulletin 1825, Washington, D.C. The ratio indicates the mean salary of this category to the mean salary of either all ranks or full professors.

decline in the relative salary position of faculty. We have already seen that real faculty salaries grew at a diminished rate in the late sixties and actually became negative in the mid-seventies. While society as a whole suffered a loss of purchasing power in the latter period, comparison of academic salaries with those of other occupations reveals that academic salaries began to fall relative to the salaries of almost all the other occupational groups presented above.

The decline in faculty salaries occured at a time when the public became disenchanted with higher education, when the rate of growth in new enrollments slowed, and when Federal funding diminished. It was accompanied by a shrinkage in the number of new positions available in academe and by a change in the career plans of new doctorates. And it has almost certainly had an impact on the reward structure of most institutions of higher education.

The chapters that follow present a more formal exploration of the nature of academic labor markets and the reward structure to which they give rise.

Notes

1. U.S. Department of Health, Education, and Welfare, *Digest of Educational Statistics*, 1974 (Washington, D. C.: Government Printing Office; 1975). The 1959-60 data are from page 84. The data for 1972-73 were obtained by telephone from W. Vance Grant, educational specialist at the Office of Education.

2. Data from W. Vance Grant.

3. *Digest of Educational Statistics*, p. 84, for early data and W. Vance Grant for 1972-73 figures.

4. *Digest of Educational Statistics*, p. 4.

5. Obtained from the National Science Foundation by telephone.

6. *Digest of Educational Statistics*, p. 110.

7. Ibid.

8. Computed from the 1967 and 1974 *Summary Reports of Doctorate Recipients from United States Universities*, prepared annually by the National Research Council, Washington, D. C.

9. The data that follow are from the 1967-1974 *Reports of Doctorate Recipients*.

10. The figures presented here are based on the AAUP average salary data, adjusted to a calendar year basis and extrapolated between years. Real growth rates are computed from changes in the consumer price index and from the two salary series.

11. The data presented here are calculated from the NEA faculty salary data shown in Table 1-2. The public school salary data may be found in National

Education Association, *Economic Status of the Teaching Profession*, Research Report 1971-74, p. 28. The 1973-74 data were obtained directly from NEA staff.

12. Evidence on this point may be found in David Brown, *The Market for College Teachers: An Economic Analysis of Career Patterns among Southeastern Social Scientists* (Durham: University of North Carolina Press, 1965).

13. The comparison is made to average, not minimum, salary, and an adjustment is made to the published figures to obtain calendar year salaries. The data come from Richard K. Yeast, "U.S. General Schedule Employees Received October 1974 Salary Increase Averaging 5.52 Percent," *Current Wage Developments*, March 1975, pp. 45-52.

2

Determinants of Academic Salaries: Alternative Views

It is better to exist than not to be at all; but existence is not the highest form of being. . . . How to be, then, not just to be–that's the question. . . . For us lesser mortals, it is at least good to know that; it is better to know how; it is best to know why.

T. V. Smith

In *The Market For College Teachers*, David Brown argues that "the determination of faculty salaries is carefully clothed in secrecy at most institutions. Time and time again, when individuals (and even department chairmen) were asked to discuss what they knew about salary determination they replied 'That stuff's top secret here' or 'That's the dean's business.' "[1] Similarly, David Katz, writing eight years later for the *American Economic Review*, points out that ". . .little is known about the process of evaluating and rewarding university professors. One possible reason may be the difficulty of obtaining good information on professors. Secondly, the analysis of such data requires a thorough knowledge of the institutional processes of wage determination. Frequently, it is difficult or impossible to obtain this data and knowledge."[2] It is ironic that although academics have studied everything from the original works of Chaucer to the gravitational pull of the moon, little has been done to provide a deterministic model of the salary determination process in academe.

Recent years have seen a sporadic outpouring of books on academe. Descriptive pieces like *The Academic Marketplace*, *The Academic Man*, and *Academic Gamesmanship* offers interesting and provocative insights into the academic reward structure.[3] Unfortunately, they fail to provide a set of hypotheses which can be used to predict the effects of changes in the academic setting, relying instead on anecdotes or personal experiences to describe the process as it exists at a given point in time.

Somewhat of an exception to this rule is David Brown's attempt to analyze academic labor markets using the concepts of supply and demand. His first effort, *The Market for College Teachers: An Economic Analysis of Career Patterns Among Southeastern Social Scientists*, involves interviews with 103 faculty members and fifty department chairmen at eighteen southeastern universities. In this work, an attempt is made to identify and examine the various components of supply and demand. Following this up with *Placement Services for College Teachers*, Brown examines the formal institutions for placement in academe, utilizing interviews with the directors of fifteen organizations.[4] A third work, *The Mobile Professors*, involves a comprehensive analysis of academic labor markets, based on the responses from a nationwide sample of newly appointed full-time faculty.[5] In this piece, Brown provides a study of the nature of the academic marketplace, the effects of job mobility, and the determinants of job choice. Since Brown has made more of a sustained effort to study academe than virtually any other economist, we begin our study of alternative theoretical views with a review of his ideas.

A Self-Contained Academic Labor Market

According to Brown, the laws of supply and demand operate in an academic labor market setting. But the process is less pure than that envisioned by the classical economist. On the demand side, labor is not paid its marginal product but rather a salary which reflects the amount available to a department for salary purposes: if a department can't find a person with the required skills at its offering price, it will reduce its skill requirements. For both budgetary and morale reasons most hiring is done at the assistant professor and instructor ranks. Senior positions are filled largely from within the institution.[6] This suggests that the forces of the marketplace have a limited effect on academic salaries at the upper levels. It also underlines the importance of subjective forces in determining faculty salaries.

Academics are assumed to be less likely to respond to changes in salary than workers in most other types of employment. Brown takes care to analyze the importance of academic salaries in attracting faculty to new positions. Citing the work of Wilson and Anantaraman, he argues that financial gain is not the prime motivation of people choosing teaching.[7] In college teaching, salary is not the measure of power, prestige, and success; other factors often substitute for salary in a person's decision to move or remain at an institution. This is especially true because large salary differences do not exist among institutions. On the basis of interview data, Brown argues, ". . .Up to a point (i.e., the minimally acceptable salary) professors are flexible less often on salary than any other job characteristics. Beyond the minimum point, salary is not determinative."[8] What this suggests is that salary may prove to be an imperfect equilibrating mechanism in equating supply and demand in the academic marketplace. However, it does not rule out salary completely as a factor influencing job choice at the margin.

Further complicating the process is the existence of balkanized academic labor markets. For Brown, "the concept of *the* academic marketplace is strictly a theoretical fetish." In reality, a series of submarkets exist, isolated from each other by type of specialization, limited search procedures, and institutional traditions such as promotion from within. Since virtually all college faculty are specialists and thus, at best, substitutable only within broad subject matter areas,

separate labor markets exist for each discipline.[9] Even between the narrowly defined disciplines, the barriers are sufficiently strong to give rise to different market conditions. Further dividing the marketplace are differences in the requirements for research by type of institution and by field, and institutional differences in the number of females and minority group members desired. Also
important are regional preferences of faculty, the prestige of the university a
faculty member comes from (especially important in gaining entry to a top 10%
department), and the prestige of the department that a person is currently at.[10]
Appointments at high prestige schools facilitate advancement through greater
specialization, better libraries and larger laboratories, reduced teaching loads,
and a host of other factors, ranging from the availability of stimulating students
to the increased opportunities for publication which exist at schools that sponsor
their own journals.[11]

What these divisions imply is that the salary determination process is not a
monolithic one and that different criteria may be important for different markets. The presence of submarkets implies that differentials will exist by field
depending on relative shortages and surpluses and that faculty will be paid a
salary that depends, at least in part, on the type of institution they attend. In
the absence of an effective information channel, faculty may end up getting
paid less than their true value.

Viewed in total, Brown's work does not provide a theoretical model of the
salary determination process but rather a set of deductive empirical studies, cast
within a supply and demand framework. While he provides a plausible explanation of why salary levels differ by field (i.e., specialization) Brown makes no
effort to contrast this explanation with others (i.e., degree of substitutability
with nonacademic positions) to test its validity. Moreover, the hypotheses presented in the three books are of limited predictive usefulness. What would be
the effect on salaries of a 100-person increase in supply? By how much would a
professor's salary rise if he or she spent more time in research? Brown tells us
that a professor will rest his job choice decision on factors such as course assignment, classroom hours, and research facilities, but what tradeoffs exist between
class hours and course assignment, between research facilities and salaries, etc.?
And why do some institutions offer faculty high salaries, low teaching hours,
and attractive facilities while others offer none of these? Brown's work serves
as a first step towards providing a set of theoretical propositions about the
workings of academic labor markets, but clearly much remains to be done.

Supply and Demand from a Broader Perspective

Using a supply-demand framework which contrasts dramatically with Brown's,
Richard B. Freeman argues that the labor market for highly trained manpower
can be explained with a simple recursive model to predict the number of PhDs

in a field at some future point.[12] In its simplest form the model consists of a
supply schedule relating the number of students entering a field to starting salaries and other incentives, a demand equation which relates the number of trained
students demanded to salary and several exogenous variables, and a market clearing equation.

The supply equation can be defined in terms of the proportion of (or amount
of) undergraduate or graduate *enrollments* or in terms of undergraduate or graduate *degrees*. Freeman defines the determinants of the supply of physicists in
terms of the initial starting salaries of new physicists (a proxy for anticipated
lifetime income), earnings available if an alternative career were chosen in lieu of
physics (represented by male professional earnings as reported by the U.S. Bureau
of the Census), and the number of physics enrollments (degrees) in the previous
period.[13]

Since the number of new entrants into a field depends on past market conditions, a number that is predetermined in relation to both the demand and
market clearing equations, Freeman argues that salary, rather than the manpower
demanded, should be the dependent variable in the demand equation.[14] Starting
salaries of BAs, MAs, and PhDs are determined by the number of graduates
(lagged one and two years) and by research and development dollars (taken as
a measure of the exogeneous demand for trained manpower and lagged one and
two periods). The presence of these lags in the demand equation insures that
faculty salaries will respond to changes in market conditions after they have
taken place. Thus, for example, shifts in Federal research funds are felt in terms
of real faculty salaries in the years following their occurrence.

An estimatable equation is obtained by plugging the demand equation into
the supply equation so that the resulting model shows the number of current
enrollments as a function of initial starting salary, alternative earnings, lagged
degrees, lagged R&D, and lagged graduates. A cobweb cycle (i.e., a cycle of
under and over response) is caused primarily by the negative impact of lagged
degrees on current enrollments.

How does Freeman's view of the labor market compare to Brown's? On
the assumption that for many "high level" labor markets the major employer
is the university, some fruitful comparisons can be made. Freeman views the
labor market in terms of supply and demand relationships. The perspective he
takes is more aggregative than Brown's, relying on the supply of students (i.e.,
enrollments) as well as the supply of people in the field to determine academic
salaries. Implicitly, this formulation rejects the notion of a balkanized labor
market, consigning the effects of such institutional practices as promotion from
within to the error term of the model. Freeman's use of the R&D variable
also gives weight to outside funding in the salary determination process, while
this variable receives only limited treatment by Brown.[15]

Freeman's salary determination equation is incomplete, lacking as it does
information on the age of faculty, their productivity, and other factors which

alter the demand for their services. These limitations may be less serious for a model dealing with manpower forecasting than for an analysis attempting to identify salary determinants by field. Nevertheless, one wonders about the potential reliability of a model which premises salary determination on only two variables.

The supply side of the model is subject to similar criticism. Given the absence of data on fellowship availability, the effects of the military draft, and family income, it is unlikely that the model will capture major long-term supply shifts. Finally, there is some evidence that the cobweb approach is applicable only to a limited number of fields.

Despite these criticisms, the Freeman model makes an important contribution to the literature. It is one of the first to explain high level manpower salaries in terms of the alternative salaries faculty can receive. This represents a major theoretical advance in the literature. Second, it links both current enrollments and salary levels to prior enrollments. This type of formulation has a strong intuitive appeal in light of the relationship implied by the data in Chapter 1. Finally, the model is cast in a deterministic framework. Small changes in a variable may be traced through to explore their consequences for both the demand and supply of professional manpower. Thus, the model has greater direct policy relevance than the studies discussed above. While its ability as a predictive tool remains to be validated, the recursive model proposed by Freeman provides a fresh perspective on a difficult problem.

A Human Capital Perspective

A quasi-theoretical view of the salary determination process in academe is found in recent work by Johnson and Stafford.[16] Concerning themselves primarily with differences in the patterns of earnings over the lifetime of academics, the authors argue that theoretical reasons exist for expecting the observed relation between earnings and experience to vary with the age at which a person begins his or her career.[17] Utilizing earlier research on the relationship between the slope of the experience-earnings curve and investment in education, they reason that "jobs with a relatively low training component must pay relatively high salaries, for an individual who takes one of these is presumably sacrificing future earnings." Who is the type of person likely to opt for a high current salary? Presumably, it is an older person who has less time to recoup the returns from a job with a large initial training component. Thus, one might expect that given two people of different ages and the same level of education, the older might opt for a job with a high initial salary while the younger might sacrifice high current income in favor of a larger future income. This implies that both starting age and experience belong in a model of salary determination.

To capture the effects of experience on earnings while controlling for differences in starting age, the authors formulate a regression equation with the natural log of academic salaries as the dependent variable and pre- and postdegree experience as the independent variables. These are entered in nonlinear form and an interaction term is included to allow for the possibility that more years of predegree experience result in a flatter postdegree earnings profile. Also included is a dummy variable to denote the sex of the respondent.

The resulting model explains more of the variation in salaries than one which does not disaggregate experience. From it, the authors reach several conclusions. First, the ratio of peak to beginning salaries is greater for those who enter an academic career early than for late starters (1.88 for PhD economists at age 25 and 1.33 for those receiving their degrees at age 35). Second, fields characterized by faculty with many years of experience have relatively flat experience-earnings profiles compared to fields whose occupants have comparatively little experience. Third, junior and senior faculty appear to be "quite substitutable in the production of instructional services, based on the estimation of a homothetic production function obtained by regressing relative supplies of faculty by field on relative salaries."[18]

Several variants of the basic model are explored. One includes an adjustment for quality of graduate school; a dummy variable denoting whether a respondent received a degree from one of the top ten graduate schools. The regression results suggest that an economist from one of the top schools averages 6% more in terms of nine-month salary than one from a non-top 10 school. However, the results also suggest that the *starting* salaries of those from top 10 schools are 5% lower than the starting salaries of those from non-top 10 schools. Thus, the earnings-experience profiles for the former are steeper.

A second variant involves separate regressions for different types of employing institutions (e.g., small private, top 20, etc.). These suggest that the research-oriented schools have steeper experience-earnings curves than the nonresearch schools, which the authors attribute in part to "differences in life cycle learning on the job and renting out one's accumulated skills."

The Johnson-Stafford findings are important in increasing our understanding of the nature of the earnings-experience relationship. What the authors fail to establish, however, is that their results are uniquely explained by human capital theory. If universities automatically grant a different salary increase each year, for example, differences in the earnings-experience profile will result simply from differences in the time when a person enters the job market. Alternatively, experience may serve as a proxy for productivity factors not included in the model. Suppose, for example, that early starters are more likely to publish than late starters, due to differences in the motivations or goals of the two groups. In this case experience might act as a proxy for other earnings-increasing activities that cumulate with age.[19] On the positive side, these findings suggest a more complete specification of the experience variable than has previously been available.

In contrast to the studies discussed so far, which are based at least in part on a theoretical framework, several studies have been conducted on a purely empirical level. Through the use of multiple regression or similar techniques, an attempt is made to quantify differences in salaries due to personal and other characteristics. The emphasis is on *quantifying* the importance of select characteristics rather than explaining *why* these affect the salary determination process. In the discussion that follows no attempt is made to provide an exhaustive compendium of research. Instead, we report the results of several studies conducted at the national level, for individual universities, and for individual departments. Our focus is on the commonalities and differences in findings among the various pieces of research.

National Data Bases

Tolles and Melichar

Of the various interdisciplinary studies at a national level, perhaps the best known is that conducted by Tolles and Melichar.[20] Using data from the National Register of Scientific and Technical Personnel, this study examines both the inter- and intraprofessional determinants of salary. To keep the discussion manageable only the 1968 findings are discussed. These are based on responses from nearly 200,000 employees in thirteen professions. It should be noted that the National Register data are obtained from a nonrandom sample of specialists in each field, that they include high-level manpower in industry and government as well as academe, and that they may involve certain methodological problems.[21] Nevertheless, they provide a fertile source of salary data by academic field which has barely been touched by researchers.

Tolles and Melichar (TM) examine the question of whether differences exist in median salary levels by academic field after allowance is made for differences in age, experience, and other factors that affect salaries. Using a regression procedure, TM regress the log of salary on the log of six salary-influencing characteristics—each characteristic being measured by a set of dummy variables—and a set of dummy variables representing the 13 academic fields. Their findings suggest that the highest academic degree variables and the years of experience and type of employer variables explain the largest amount of the variation in the data (0.159 and 0.149 respectively), followed by the profession variable (.066), primarily work activity variables (.065), sex (.024), and age (.019).[22] If the explanatory power of a particular characteristic is measured gross of the effects of other variables, several dramatic shifts occur in the ordering discussed above. The experience-type of employer variables explain the largest amount of variation in the data (0.34), followed by age (0.24) and primary work activity (.146). Highest academic degree and profession explain only .065 and .017 of the variation, and sex accounts for .037. These reversals suggest that the independent variables used in the regression are not orthogonal.

The TM study represents one of the first national attempts to identify the determinants of academic salaries for different fields.[23] While its central purpose is to analyze the salaries of economists and to relate these to the salaries of other professionals, it provides several insights into the role of the balkanized markets described by Brown. For example, TM find that those in management earn 17% more than those in research and 27% more than those in teaching.[24] Likewise, females earn 16% less than males. Even within a given field, economists in some specialities earn more than those in others. For example, those in monetary and fiscal theory earn 3.7% more than the national geometric mean salary for economists, while those in land economics earn 6.8% less.

The Cohn Study

An alternative approach to the problem is proposed by Cohn.[25] Using sample data from 204 institutions reporting data on salaries and other faculty compensation to the AAUP, Cohn attempts to explain differences in the average salary of faculty at each rank in the 1970-71 academic year. Thirteen explanatory variables are considered, including three variables for type of institution (university, private independent, church), one denoting whether the institution is in the Northeast, one for number of merit scholars, one for the proportion of students pursuing graduate or professional education, one for the student/faculty ratio and for the percent change in this ratio respectively, one for enrollment and enrollment squared respectively, one for percent of faculty holding the full professor rank, one representing per capita income in the state where the school is located, and one for an AAUP classification II school. A separate set of regressions is also run using average salary plus "other compensation" as the dependent variable. No defense is given for the particular set of variables chosen except that they "characterize both demand and supply aspects of the market for college faculty." Moreover, the author includes no discussion of the aggregation biases implicit in the use of the institution as the basis for analysis or of the direction of bias introduced by the nonrandom selection procedure he employs in his study.

Cohn's model introduces two sets of variables not usually found in salary determination models, and both have fairly large t-values. The first, a set of nonlinear terms for enrollment, enters the individual rank equations with t-values ranging from 2.25 to 5.17. (Note that the statistical significance of the squared enrollment term raises doubts as to the validity of the linear term employed by Freeman.) One wonders, however, whether enrollments should enter the salary determination equation directly, or indirectly through their effects on the criteria different sized institutions use to reward faculty. And it seems clear that a lag structure such as that proposed by Freeman would have more intuitive appeal than a variable relating student enrollments in the current year to current salaries.[26]

The second variable, per capita income in the state where the school is located (lagged two years), enters the regression equations for the individual ranks with t-values ranging from 4.51 to 6.00. Cohn makes no attempt to explain whether this is a supply, demand, or reduced-form variable, or why he uses 1969 rather than 1971 data. While the strong statistical showing for this variable suggests that it might be useful in aggregate studies, a stronger case needs to be made at a theoretical level before it is included. If it is a supply variable then why is it included separately in an equation with enrollments? If it enters on the demand side, perhaps as a proxy for ability to pay, then why is it used in place of a more direct measure of institutional wealth? On these and similar questions, the author remains silent.[27]

Although Cohn's work suggests that reasonable results can be obtained by researchers interested in explaining interinstitutional variation in salary, it is not clear that models of this type are useful from a policy perspective. For one thing, they wash out the intrainstitutional variation discussed in the next section. For another, the purposes served by explaining institutional variations in average salaries are not clear. While such models might be useful for the types of comparative analyses conducted by the AAUP, the aggregate equation proposed by Cohn fails to capture the effects of qualitative differences, of age, productivity, and composition of faculty. Thus it provides only limited insights into the true sources of interinstitutional differences.

Studies of Individual Institutions

The arguments in support of widespread differences in the salary determination practices of individual institutions are quite strong. Earlier we reported on Brown's findings that the academic labor market is balkanized and on the Johnson-Stafford finding that different earnings-experience profiles are obtained depending on one's choice of schools. What these findings suggest is that the coefficient values obtained in the national studies are sensitive to the choice of sample. Less clear is the question of whether the determinants of salaries differ at various types of institutions. One way to answer this question is to partition a national sample by institutional type and to develop separate salary determination models; a second way is to consider the findings of researchers studying the determinants of salaries at individual institutions.

In this section, we examine three studies of the salary determination process for individual institutions. Two of these involve universities which place emphasis on publications, presumably as a measure of productivity; the third university emphasizes teaching and appears to give little value to faculty publications.

Since the methodology employed by the authors differs, direct comparisons of their results are not possible. An attempt is made to highlight commonalities in their research whenever possible.

The Katz Study

In a recent study, David Katz examines the factors he believes to be important in salary and promotion decisionmaking at a large "highly ranked" public university.[28] Working with personal interviews with chairmen or heads of departments of nine of the eleven departments included in his study, Katz found that most agreed that "research ability, publication record, and national reputation were the most important factors influencing salary and promotion decisions." Research ability was measured primarily by examining the quality of journals in which publications appeared and by book reviews. Also weighed in the process were public service to both the community and the university.

Armed with this information, Katz formulated a linear regression in which academic-year salary was regressed on a set of independent variables. These include: number of books published, number of articles published, number of articles published in the best journals, whether the professor was ranked in the top 50% of instructors by students, number of dissertations supervised since 1964, hours per week devoted to public service, hours devoted to committee assignments, and number of years since highest degree. A set of dummy variables is also employed, including D_1 = 1 if person is a political scientist, D_2 = 1 if person is a physical or laboratory scientist, D_3 = 1 if person is in the humanities, D_4 = 1 if person is in English, U_1 = 1 if person received an undergraduate degree from a school containing the top 10% of all faculty, U_2 = 1 if person received an undergraduate degree from a school with the next 70% of faculty, U_3 = 1 if from bottom 20%, U_4 = 1 if from foreign or unranked school, G = 1 if person received a graduate degree from the bottom group of graduate departments, M = 1 if person had an administrative assignment, X = 1 if person is female, N = 1 if person held an eleven-month appointment, R = 1 if person has a PhD.[29]

Several of the findings reported by Katz are quite interesting. A rough guess based on the size of the F-values reported in his table suggests that the experience variable probably explains the largest amount of variation in the data. Also entering with large F-values are the dissertations supervised and the sex variables. Virtually all of the dummy variables for field are found to be statistically significant, a phenomenon explained by Katz in terms of "possible differences in market supply and demand" for the various disciplines.[30] The administration variable, Katz's equivalent for the Tolles and Melichar work activities variables, enters with a significant and large positive regression coefficient ($2,557). Thus Katz's research suggests that many of the variables significant for the national level are also significant for a single institution.[31]

Especially interesting in this study are the findings with respect to the role of publications in the salary process. Katz finds that each article published by a faculty member adds $18 to his or her annual salary, each book adds $230, and each "excellent article" adds $102. These figures seem implausibly low given the length of time required to prepare a publication and the findings from other studies.[32] Katz acknowledges that the linear form of his model may be a problem and provides select estimates of the returns to publication, presumably obtained by including nonlinear publication terms. This procedure is suspect, however, because of the likelihood that a nonlinear experience variable should have been included in the model. (Recall that both the Tolles and Melichar and Johnson and Stafford studies suggest that experience affects salary in a nonlinear fashion.)

Katz presents a finding that appears to be validated by several studies discussed in this chapter, namely, that publication is rewarded by universities while teaching is not. As we shall see, the validity of this finding rests with the specific institution considered. He also finds that quality of undergraduate school is not a significant predictor of salary while quality of graduate school is: those from the top-rated graduate schools earn $850 more than those in less well regarded departments. These results are supportive of those of Johnson and Stafford, and they suggest that many of the same variables that affect salaries at a national level also affect salaries at individual institutions.

The Koch and Chizmar Study

The work of Koch and Chizmar stands in contrast to that of Katz.[33] Examining data on 229 professors in sixteen academic departments at Illinois State University, the authors present a salary determination model that includes experience, sex, race, degree status, and a set of merit evaluations dealing with teaching ability, scholarly productivity, and public service. Also included in the model are a set of dummy variables denoting academic rank and a set of variables reflecting whether the external market for a given discipline is "very weak," "moderately weak," or "moderately strong." These are used to explain both absolute salaries and salary increments. What the authors find is that teaching competence is the most important determinant of salary *increments*, followed by scholarly activity, service, and committee activity. The most significant determinants of *absolute* salary levels are academic rank and experience. Factors such as teaching ability, research ability, and public service explain about 20% of the variation in salaries, compared to the 90% explained by the addition of rank, experience, race, etc.

While the limited nature of the Koch and Chizmar study makes it difficult to evaluate, it is probably true that predominantly undergraduate institutions place less weight on publications than the highly ranked graduate institutions. Especially interesting is the robustness of the experience variable which is underscored by all of the studies reported in this section. Note too, the consistent finding of lower salaries for females.

The Ferber Study

In a frontal attack on the question of whether sex influences the reward structure
of academe, Marianne Ferber examined the salary structure of 278 faculty at the
University of Illinois (Urbana-Champaign) employed during the 1969-70 academic
year.[34] Using a stepwise multiple correlation procedure, she predicted salaries
for men and women separately in a series of equations. The first included length
of appointment (i.e., nine or eleven months), experience, number of professional
honors, highest academic degree, and papers read at meetings. The results con-
firm those reported earlier regarding experience and highest degree, but they do
not reflect a statistically significant difference in salaries according to length of
appointment. When the department's mean salary at the rank corresponding to
the person's is introduced in the model together with years at current rank, bul-
letins published, books written and edited, and spouse employed at the University of Illinois (a dummy variable), dramatic differences emerge in the set of
variables predicting salaries for men and women. While all of the variables ex-
cepting marital status and papers read at meetings are significant predictors of
men's salaries, only mean salary of the person's rank in department, length of
appointment, papers read at meetings, and marital status are significant predictors of female salaries. Ferber concludes that scholarly productivity does
not "bear heavily" on within-rank salary differences, that years in rank is important in determining men's salaries but *not* women's, and that married faculty
women are both paid less than single women and have husbands who are paid
less than other male faculty. These findings suggest that given a differential
reward structure for men and women, studies aggregating the two sexes are
of somewhat limited predictive value.

Gordon, Morton, and Braden

Further evidence of the effect of sex on the reward structure of academe is provided in a recent study of virtually all full-time academic employees of a large
urban university conducted by Gordon, Morton, and Braden (GMB).[35] The
authors regress salary on age, race, years at the university, current education,
rank, and department, both separately and for all faculty combined. The data
are for the 1970-71 academic year and include between 1,000 and 2,000 employees (an exact number is not reported to preserve the anonymity of the university). In contrast to the models presented earlier, GMB use a piecewise age
function which is introduced to isolate nonlinear effects. They also exclude
variables that might measure differences in the productivity of faculty.

GMB find that women's salaries peak earlier than men's. Men's salaries
increase at approximately 0.6% per year until age 45, rise more slowly (0.1%
per year) until age 55, and then decrease at about 0.2% per year. In contrast,
women's salaries rise by 0.9% per year until age 35, remain the same until 45,

decrease at about 1.4% per year between ages 45 and 55, and remain the same thereafter. On the average, men's salaries peak about fifteen years after women's. In the absence of better productivity measures, it is difficult to interpret the causes for these differences but they may reflect at least some discrimination. Differences between men and women are also found in the race and academic-field variables. Taken in total, GMB argue that a female faculty member earns between 9.5% and 11.4% less than a corresponding male faculty member, depending on whether the sex of the faculty member is included directly in a single regression or used to partition the data into separate equations.

It appears that the traditional salary determination variables described above do not have the same effects for women as they do for men. This is the implication of the GMB study, and it is supported by a recent national study by Johnson and Stafford.[36] It raises a serious objection to the other studies discussed in this chapter. If the salary determinants for females differ from those of males, then separate regression equations should be run for men and women; studies treating sex as a dummy variable that raises or lowers some intercept value probably obscure both the importance and the nature of sex differences in the salary determination process. We explore this point in greater detail in chapter 4.

A Salary Determination Model for a Single Department

It is useful to contrast the findings for a single department with those at the institutional and national level. Use of an individual department avoids the need to control for variations in salary level by institution, by geographic region, by condition of the market for PhDs in different fields, etc. Of course, the findings from studies of this type are difficult to generalize.

Siegfried and White (SW), using data on 45 economists at the University of Wisconsin, postulate a simple salary determination model that includes years of experience, number of monographs, articles in national journals of a general nature, articles in speciality and regional journals, all other publications (textbooks, edited books, etc.), a variable measuring student evaluation of faculty teaching, and a dummy variable for whether the faculty member has held a major administrative position at the university.[37] These variables are used to explain the 1971-72 academic year salary of faculty. The authors find that all of the independent variables are statistically significant at the .01 level with the exception of the teaching performance variable (significant at the .10 level) and monographs, which are not statistically significant. As one might expect, the experience variable enters the regression with a reasonably large t-value (4.24) and a coefficient of $253.[38] Administrative duties increase the salary of the average faculty member by $5,208 (t-value of 6.45), and outstanding teaching barely affects faculty salary ($731 increase, t-value of 1.70).[39] The SW findings on the returns to article publication suggest a salary increment of $392 for articles in national general journals, $344 for national specialty journals, and $76 for other publications. Monographs do not increase the salary of faculty members.

The SW study is important for several reasons. First it suggests that the salary determination process is at least partially rational even at the level of the individual department. The variables listed above explain about 88% of the variation in salary levels. Second, it highlights the importance of publications in determining differences in salaries among faculty. While it would have been useful if SW had included information on public service, dissertations supervised, advising, and other activities, the strong showing of the publications variables suggests that, at least for the Wisconsin Economics Department, they play an important role in determining salaries. Third, the results suggest that work activity and experience are important salary determinants at virtually all levels, from the department (as reported by SW) to the national level (as suggested by Tolles and Melichar).

Summary

Despite a proliferation of salary determination "models," surprisingly little theory underlies the work on the determinants of salaries in academe. In part, this is due to the character of the academic labor market. Outputs are not well defined, academic institutions are multiproduct firms, and hiring decisions may be characterized by second-best decisionmaking. In part, too, it is due to the sparsity of detailed national data sources amenable to rigorous analysis and hypothesis formation.

Theoretical approaches have been formulated by David Brown, Richard Freeman, and George Johnson and Frank Stafford. These differ in perspective; the first study focuses solely on the demand and supply of college faculty, while the second relates the demand for faculty to the supply of students and indirectly the market for college services. The third study focuses solely on a human-capital explanation of how faculty salaries change through time. Each approach offers what appear to be valid insights into the nature of the salary determination process, but none provides an all-encompassing framework that can be used to build a common foundation for future studies.

Despite the absence of a theoretical explanation of the operation of academic labor markets, recent years have seen a substantial increase in the number of empirical studies based on "salary determination models." These are essentially single equation regression models based largely on intuition. Interestingly, they show a remarkable consistency in terms of which variables cause academic salaries to differ. Perhaps the most important of these is the number of years of experience a faculty member has. It is not known whether this variable reflects institutional practices (rewarding employees for longevity), a measure of the returns to human-capital accumulation, or the demand-supply conditions existing at different points in time. But the repeated confirmation of the role of experience suggests that studies of the type conducted by Johnson and Stafford and Gordon, Morton, and Braden are cumulative.

Less clear are the findings with respect to the role of other variables. At least two studies suggest that the salary determination process for females differs from that of males. In both cases, no allowance is made for differences in productivity, in quality of graduate institution, in work activity, and in other work-related characteristics. Thus, while it may be true that a female faculty member earns less than her male counterpart, these studies make a weak argument for this finding. Likewise, the evidence as to the returns to researchers as compared to teachers, is mixed. Several studies find that publishers receive significantly more than teachers, but others suggest that this might not be true for all institutions. Finally, the evidence is at least somewhat mixed as to the relationship between the quality of the person's prior training, the quality of the person's current institution, and the level of his or her academic salary.

Notes

1. David G. Brown, *The Market for College Teachers: An Economic Analysis of Career Patterns among Southeastern Social Scientists* (Durham: University of North Carolina Press, 1965), p. 154. Hereafter referred to as *College Teachers.*

2. David A. Katz, "Faculty Salaries, Promotions, and Productivity at a Large University," *American Economic Review* 63 (June 1973):469.

3. Theodore Caplow and Reece J. McGee, *The Academic Marketplace* (New York: Basic Books, 1958), Logan Wilson, *The Academic Man: A Study in the Sociology of a Profession* (New York: Oxford University Press, 1942), Pierre van den Berghe, *Academic Gamesmanship* (New York: Abelard-Schuman, 1970).

4. David G. Brown, *Placement Services for College Teachers,* a report to U.S. Department of Labor, Office of Manpower, Automation and Training (Washington, D.C.: Government Printing Office, 1965).

5. David G. Brown, *The Mobile Professor* (Washington, D.C.: American Council on Education, 1967).

6. Brown, *College Teachers,* p. 55.

7. Wilson, *The Academic Man,* p. 136, and Venkatraman Anantaraman, *Mobility of Professional Economists in the United States* (Madison: University of Wisconsin, Industrial Relations Section, 1961), pp. 5,7.

8. Brown, *College Teachers,* p. 230.

9. Brown, *The Mobile Professors,* pp. 62-63, 66.

10. Ibid., pp. 94-103.

11. These differences in prestige seem to give rise to a desire on the part of young faculty to start at the top, even at a reduced salary, since according to Brown, most movement in academe takes place in a downward direction.

12. Richard B. Freeman, "Supply and Salary Adjustments to the Changing Science Manpower Market: Physics, 1948-1973," *American Economic Review* 65 (March 1975):27-39.

13. The author experiments with alternative lag periods. Because the inclusion of a lagged dependent variable in the equation reduces the salary coefficient substantially, he argues for the existence of different short- and long-run elasticities of supply. Both degrees and enrollments are used for the lagged variable.

14. Freeman, "Supply and Salary Adjustments," p. 31.

15. It is likely that R&D has played a more important role in setting salaries for the sciences than it has for the humanities or the social sciences. This may explain the difference in treatment by the two authors.

16. George E. Johnson and Frank P. Stafford, "Lifetime Earnings in a Professional Labor Market: Academic Economists," *Journal of Political Economy*, 82 (May/June 1974): 549-569. Hereafter footnoted as "Lifetime Earnings."

17. By assumption, skills acquired in unrelated past work are treated as not transferable to present occupations.

18. The dependent variable is the log of the ratio of the number of faculty in a field with fourteen or more years of experience to the number of faculty with less than fourteen years of experience. The independent variable is the log of the ratio of the salaries of those with fourteen or more years of experience to the salaries of those with less than fourteen years of experience.

19. The R^2s reported by Johnson and Stafford are generally fairly low for the aggregated equations and are as high as 0.79 for the University of California disaggregation. It should be noted that the California schools are subject to fairly careful legislative regulation of salaries based on years in rank.

20. N. Arnold Tolles and Emanuel Melichar, "Studies of the Structure of Economists' Salaries and Income," *American Economic Review*, 58 (Supplement) (December 1968) (hereafter referred to as National Register), and "The Structure of Economists' Employment and Salaries, 1964," *American Economic Review*, 55 (Supplement) (December 1964).

21. For a discussion of the limitations of these data, see John K. Folger, Helen S. Astin, and Alan E. Bayer, *Human Resources and Higher Education* (New York: Russell Sage, 1970), Appendix D.

22. These are the partial R^2s obtained by including all of the characteristics in the model.

23. The interested reader may wish to contrast the findings of the earlier 1964 study with those of A.G. Holtmann and Alan E. Bayer, "Determinants of Professional Income among Recent Recipients of National Science Doctorates," *Journal of Business* 43 (October 1970), and Barbara and Howard Tuckman, "The Structure of Salaries at American Universities," *Journal of Higher Education* 47 (January 1976).

24. Recall that these work-activity categories include people outside of the academic marketplace because of the nature of the sample.

25. Elchanan Cohn, "Factors Affecting Variations in Faculty Salaries and Compensation in Institutions of Higher Education," *Journal of Higher Education* 44 (February 1973): 124-135.

26. Cohn uses lagged data for the number of National Merit Scholars and the percentage of students pursuing a graduate education. It is not clear, however, whether this is done for theoretical reasons or whether it is the result of data-gathering problems.

27. For example, the author finds that it makes little difference whether the dependent variable is average salary alone or average salary plus other forms of compensation. The R^2s on his two sets of equations range between 0.02 and 0.04 apart, and the t-values for both equations are quite similar. Does this mean that either measure is appropriate or that one is superior to another? He does not tell us. Likewise, given the nature of his data, one wonders about the problem of heteroscedasticity, yet no mention is made of this in his paper.

28. Katz, "Faculty Salaries," pp. 469-477.

29. A dummy variable is a variable that assumes a value of 1 if the faculty member has this attribute and a 0 otherwise. The regression coefficients obtained for these variables represent additions or subtractions from the intercept term.

30. D_1 is used as the reference group and included in the intercept term.

31. Sex, PhD degree, and eleven-month contract, variables also considered by Tolles and Melichar, are significant in the Katz regression.

32. For a contrasting set of estimates, see Howard P. Tuckman and Jack Leahey, "What Is an Article Worth?" *Journal of Political Economy* 83 (October 1975): 951-968.

33. James V. Koch and John F. Chizmar, "The Influence of Teaching and Other Factors upon Absolute Salaries and Salary Increments at Illinois State University," *Journal of Economic Education*, Fall 1973, pp. 27-34.

34. Marianne A. Ferber, "Professors, Performance, and Rewards," *Industrial Relations* 13, no. 1, pp. 67-79.

35. Nancy M. Gordon, Thomas E. Morton, and Ina C. Braden, "Faculty Salaries: Is There Discrimination by Sex, Race, and Discipline?" *American Economic Review* 64 (June 1974): 419-427.

36. George E. Johnson and Frank P. Stafford, "The Earnings and Promotion of Women Faculty," *American Economic Review* 64 (December 1974): 888-903. In this study the authors find that the salaries of academic females start out between 4% and 11% less than those of academic males. Over the years they decline on a relative basis, falling to 13% to 23% of that of males fifteen years after the doctorate is completed. This implies a different return to experience than is obtained by academic males.

37. John J. Siegfried and Kenneth J. White, "Teaching and Publishing as Determinants of Academic Salaries," *Journal of Economic Education* 5 (Spring 1973): 90-99.

38. Regrettably, Siegfried and White do not indicate the effects of treating experience in a nonlinear fashion.

39. If this comment seems surprising, recall that good teaching may have a one-time effect on salary while *each* article a person writes has a salary-increasing effect.

3 The Interrelatedness of
Academic Markets

Words move, music moves
Only in time; but that which is only living can only die.
Words, after the speech, reach
Into the silence. Only by the form, the pattern, can words or music reach. . . .
                                                              T.S. Eliot

The cross-section studies discussed in the last chapter are helpful in understanding the salary differentials that currently exist in academe, and we shall use
this methodological approach in the following chapters. Before doing so, it is
useful to look at a conceptual model that provides an understanding of the
dynamic and interactive nature of the salary determination and reward systems.
In the process, the limitations of the cross-section approach will become more
obvious.

An Overview of the Conceptual Model

Figure 3-1 presents the conceptual model discussed in this chapter. The lefthand
side shows the three educational product markets and the determinants of
demand and supply for these markets. The outcomes of the operation of these
markets are translated, through appropriate constraints, into a set of demands for
faculty time. These demands (indicated by the dark unbroken lines) interact in
the academic labor markets with the supply of faculty time (the supply side is
depicted by a broken set of lines) to establish an equilibrium price and time
allocation for alternative skill categories.

The academic reward structure is shown on the right side of the figure. The
top and right sides of the box show the major inputs into the process and the
bottom shows the outputs, most of which draw faculty away from those
activities directly related to product market demands.

The figure illustrates the basic interdependence between the academic
product and labor markets and the set of institutional rules and rewards established by the universities and professional associations to which faculty belong.
Economic events affect the salaries offered to faculty, the way faculty allocate
their time at the margin, and the academic reward structure. The reward
structure creates a set of pecuniary and nonpecuniary incentives which may
either reinforce or offset the financial incentives created by the operation of

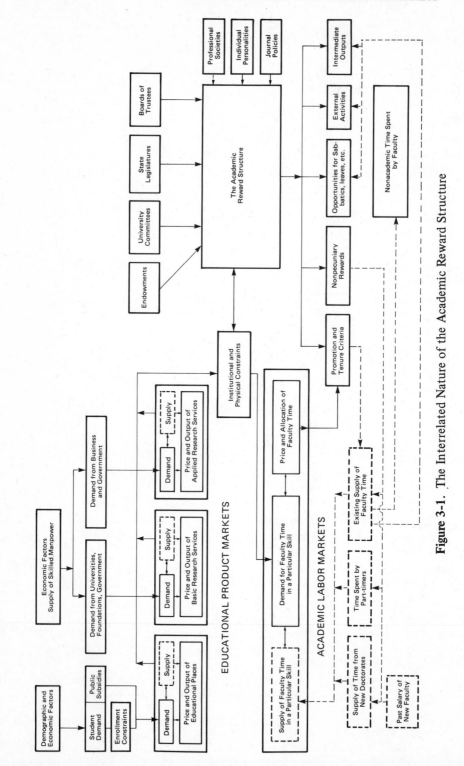

Figure 3-1. The Interrelated Nature of the Academic Reward Structure

the academic labor markets. The two systems interact and change through time, creating the differentials discussed in the last chapter.

The Educational Services Product Market

Our analysis begins with the market for educational services. Here the demanders of services interact with the institutions that supply them. It may be that the real world involves many more markets than are shown here. For example, Brown and others argue that separate markets exist for the services of religious institutions, of prestige institutions, of those catering to women, etc.[1] However, the basic structure shown in the figure remains unchanged if more components are added. The academic product markets consist of demanders and suppliers. As a result of their interaction, and subject to institutional constraints, the price and quantity of educational services is determined.

Institutions of higher education are asked to provide three basic types of educational services. These include the transmission of knowledge (represented by the market for educational places), the creation and development of new knowledge (represented by the market for basic research), and the application of knowledge (represented by the market for contractual work, consulting, and public service). Educational institutions may provide services to their clientele other than those presented above, but these are primarily by-products and will be ignored for present purposes.[2] The three types of services are not easily distinguished and in practice may be joint products. Nevertheless, the conceptual distinction between the markets is a useful one.

The demand for educational services depends on several economic and demographic variables; psychological variables probably also affect student demand, but these are difficult to distinguish at an aggregate level. Evidence from a variety of studies suggests that the demand for higher education depends on family income, the cost of obtaining an education, and the occupational and educational background of household heads.[3] Less well defined is the role of the expected future returns to higher education.

The determinants of the supply of educational places are less well known. In the 1700s and early 1800s, the supply of colleges (and therefore of places) was related to the educational aspirations of various religious groups. Later in the century, the number of colleges expanded as a result of land grant legislation. More recently, the supply of new places appears to have been responsive to changes in the demand for places, with enrollment constraints imposed in lieu of price increases to handle excess demand.[4] The actions of state legislatures have also played an important role.[5]

Surprisingly little research has been conducted on the determinants of the demand and supply of basic and applied research. The quantity of these services demanded is probably related to the real rate of growth of gross national product (a proxy for the prosperity of the various levels of government and the foundations), prior levels of public R&D expenditure, and expectations about society's future need for manpower trained in research. But most universities and some prestige colleges generate their own demand for research through internal grants, the creation of research institutes, and reward structures that favor those engaged in research.

The supply of basic and applied research depends upon the number of faculty available with a desired set of skills, the returns to these skills, and the alternative demands on faculty time. A substantial increase in the demand for faculty time in one market (i.e., the market for teaching) is likely to be met by a reduction in the time available to supply services in the other markets.

The market relations described above are difficult to formulate along the optimization lines favored by many economists.[6] They are amenable to mathematical modeling, however, and a serious effort to construct this type of model is needed. The problem is that time-series data are not currently available to provide a test of the predictive accuracy of such a model. However, cross-section evidence on the existing allocation of faculty time will be presented in Chapter 7.

The Link between the Two Markets

Conventional economic theory suggests that if two markets are perfectly competitive, the demand curve in the resource market will be derived from the supply curve in the corresponding product market. The slope and corresponding elasticity of the resource demand curve are defined by a production function which specifies the relationship between the inputs of resources and the output of goods.

The difficulty in applying conventional economic theory to the higher education area is that in the absence of a widely held and uniformly applied learning theory, an educational production function cannot be assumed to exist.[7] For example, an increase in enrollments may be met by an increase in the number of new faculty hired, by an increase in the average student-faculty ratio, or by greater use of student teachers. Little is known about the consequences of each alternative, and thus we are unable to define an optimum set of inputs that IHEs should employ. In deference to our ignorance, the link between the two markets is labeled "institutional and physical constraints" in Figure 3-1. Note that the relationship between the two markets can be altered by changes in the academic reward structure.

Monetary Returns to Particular Skills

Since the supply of new faculty is inelastic in the short run, an increase in the demand for a particular service is likely to increase the salary of those currently possessing the skills to provide that service. It is also likely to increase the time faculty spend acquiring this skill. Among the most often discussed skills are those of teaching, research, public service, and administration, although it is likely that other skills are also important.

The time available to faculty to pursue alternative activities is limited by the length of their day and their physical stamina. Thus, the additional time spent in an activity as a result of an increase in the return to engaging in that activity may be limited in the short run.[8] Changes in the mix of educational services demanded may help to explain the salary differentials observed in the last chapter. For example, the increase in the demand for researchers during the sixties may have bid up the salaries of those with research skills. To the extent that this was the case, the decline in the demand for research in the 1970s seems to suggest that a decline in the relative salaries of researchers is likely.

Most departments would like to employ faculty skilled in research, teaching, and public service. These skills can potentially provide a variety of returns, including increases in student enrollments, outside grant funding, and recognition by the university and local community. But most faculty do not possess these skills in equal measure. Given limited resources, departments can hire only a few faculty, and choices must be made from among those available. Which faculty member a department chooses will depend on the importance it gives to the package of skills offered by each potential faculty member and on the price of these skills in the marketplace.[9] Tenure regulations limit a department's ability to adjust to changes in demand by altering the skills of its existing faculty members. Thus, changes in the existing skill mix of a department are likely to occur slowly.

Good teachers are often not the best researchers, and those skilled in public service may be poor administrators. Since each skill takes time to develop, faculty must to some extent choose among competing uses of their time. The return they expect to receive will at least partially affect which skills they acquire. Of course, faculty will also be influenced by where their comparative advantage lies, by their past experience, and by a host of other factors. But this does not preclude the possibility that financial returns affect behavior at the margin.

If the demand for a given skill increases, the salary increment paid to faculty with this skill will increase in the short run; this creates a differential among facult; with different sets of skills. In the long run, the number of faculty possessing the desired skill increases, and this tends to lower the differential among faculty.[10]

Several types of skills may be distinguished and valued by the academic marketplace. These include area specializations such as those offered by clinical psychologists, plastic surgeons, ethnomethodologists, or microbiologists.[11] They also include the specialities that faculty acquire by spending time in an activity. For example, an outstanding teacher is usually a person who has taken the time to prepare his lecture notes carefully and to develop a set of effective teaching techniques.

To the extent that the development of each skill requires a unique set of inputs, the elasticity of supply for the skills will differ. For example, a large increase in the return to teaching may bring forth large amounts of additional time spent in teaching. In contrast, at least in the short run, an equivalent increase in the returns to basic research may bring forth a relatively smaller amount of additional effort if there are fewer people with research skills available or if research skills take longer to acquire. How much of the differential across academic fields is explained by differences in the skill requirements for these fields is not known; it seems clear that such differences are important, however.

Several caveats should be noted concerning the preceding analysis. Immobilities may result in some faculty's receiving less than their worth in the competitive marketplace. Those who remain in one department for several years often find their salaries determined primarily by the processes prevailing in those departments. Insulation from the operation of the national labor markets may thus lead to lower-than-market returns to particular skills. Likewise, some faculty who allow their skills to languish may receive higher returns for their skills in their own departments than they would receive in the national labor markets.[12]

The academic labor markets probably approximate the perfectly competitive model most closely at the assistant professor level.[13] This is because the supply of new faculty hired from the national labor markets is likely to be greatest at this rank and because the lack of tenure of most assistants enables institutions to hire or fire them fairly easily. It may also reflect the operation of such institutionalized procedures as promotion from within and the structuring of salaries to preserve within-rank equities. Fringe benefit policies which lock in older faculty to their institutions also have an effect.

Nonpecuniary rewards may act to offset the effects of market incentives. For example, some faculty choose an academic job over a higher-paying job elsewhere because they like to teach. Over some salary range, their allocation of time to alternative activities may be unresponsive to changes in the relative returns to teaching, reflecting the satisfactions they receive from teaching. Beyond the point where the lower return to teaching causes more dissatisfaction than teaching creates satisfaction, faculty may begin to cultivate alternative skills.

What these caveats suggest is that the returns to a particular skill may not be determined in an optimal fashion by the academic marketplace and that the process may allow some faculty to gain excess rents while others receive less than their market value. But as long as the academic markets create a differential return to individual skills, they also create an incentive structure which may affect faculty behavior.

Nondirect Effects of the Academic Reward Structure

The markets discussed above are directly influenced by economic variables. But the operation of these markets is modified and shaped by the set of institutional rules and policies that we have dubbed the academic reward structure. Included in this classification are the promotion and tenure process, the returns to academic activities outside the university, and the rewards to nonacademic activity.

Promotion and tenure decisions play an important role in defining the mix of skills available at a point in time in academe. These decisions are necessarily subjective since they involve expectations as to the future skill mix needed by departments, estimates of the ability of departments to obtain faculty with more desirable skill packages than are currently employed, and appraisals as to the intensity of the skills offered by the faculty under consideration. This gatekeeper process partially defines the set of skills available within academe and directly affects the academic reward structure by assigning a set of survival probabilities to alternative uses of faculty time. These issues are analyzed in greater detail in Chapter 6. For present purposes, it is useful to note that the promotion and tenure process is largely internally defined and that it tends both to modify and be modified by the outcomes of the operation of the product and labor markets.

The educational outputs discussed at the beginning of this chapter represent the end-products purchased by users. But a number of intermediate products are also produced by faculty which are consumed by other faculty in their production of the three types of services. These include the critiquing of papers written by other faculty, referee and editorial services to the academic journals, offices in professional societies, honorary positions in such learned groups as the National Academy of Sciences, etc. Time expended in these directions usually implies less time for other activities. Nonetheless, these activities may offer considerable nonpecuniary rewards to faculty. Little is known about the determinants of the supply and demand for these activities.

A third set of factors affecting the allocation of faculty time are the nondirect academic activities in which faculty engage. These include such things as the publication of principles textbooks, outside consulting on problems related to the subjects taught by faculty, etc. The opportunities faculty have to engage in these activities depend on their geographic location, reputation, and areas of expertise. It seems reasonable to assume that as the return to this type of activity rises relative to the return to other time uses, faculty time in other activities falls.

Outside Income and the Academic Reward Structure

The existence and survival of the academic reward structure can be explained above, at least in part, by the imperfect nature of the educational markets. The demanders of educational places are largely uninformed about the appropriate mix of courses, faculty, and other educational inputs. This gives educators an important say, over the technology employed by and the rewards given to faculty. Likewise, much research is financed either directly through grants initiated by individual faculty or through release time provided by the faculty member's employing institution. This allows faculty some control over the direction their research will take. The less direct the tie between the funding source and the educational marketplace, the greater the likelihood that the academic reward structure will have an impact in defining faculty behavior.

Further influencing the independence of the reward structure is the availability of funds unrelated to the demand for specific services. These may be alumni gifts or interest from endowments; they may also be oil royalties, other income from assets, spillovers from operating accounts such as the athletic fund, or unearmarked funds from a state legislature.

An increase (decrease) in outside funds is likely to be at least partially used to increase (decrease) the supply of faculty, other things being equal. Outside funds may also be used to reduce the average time that faculty spend in teaching, increase the time spent in research, and/or upgrade the average quality of faculty at those institutions where such funds are available.[14] The availability of these funds at least partially creates the opportunity for a reward structure to develop independently of market demands. To the extent that the reward structure rewards innovation, quality of work, and other positives, such independence is highly desirable. To the extent that it makes educational institutions less responsive to the markets they serve, it may be undesirable.

In either case, it seems clear that efforts designed to change the directions taken by modern institutions of higher education are likely to fail unless they take the academic reward structure into account. This is true of the voucher schemes recently proposed to finance higher education; and it is equally true for the myriad of control systems employed by boards of regents. A competent administrator cannot afford to ignore the incentive effects of his or her policies.

Implications of the Model

The analysis presented above gives rise to several insights of interest to students of academic labor markets. First, the process is made up of both market and non-market elements, and its outcomes reflect the interrelationships between the two sets of forces. Second, the salary process is partially deterministic, and as such it gives rise to specific generalizations as to the outcomes emerging from specific policy changes. Finally, the salary differentials reported in the last chapter represent a set of outcomes that depend on the economic, demographic, and institutional conditions prevailing at a given point in time.

To the extent that the process is made up of both market and nonmarket elements, it seems clear that university administrators have some freedom to alter faculty behavior through their manipulation of the policies and rules that underlie the promotion and tenure process, new hires, and the internal system of rewards. Although the point may seem obvious, many administrators do not recognize that the rules they make affect the allocation of time by faculty at the margin.

The deterministic side of the salary determination process is frequently ignored by students of the process in favor of the subjective decisions that occasionally characterize it. This is unfortunate because it impedes the development of a model capable of quantifying the impact of alternative policies and economic outcomes. Recent years have seen a substantial increase in the use of such models for evaluating the consequences of alternative Federal policies in the health and welfare areas. The field of education may be a suitable next candidate for the application of models of this type.

Cross-Section Studies and the Conceptual Model

Cross-section studies are useful for several purposes. They provide information to educational policymakers on what the average reward structure looks like. This may in turn suggest where changes can be made. They also provide a standard against which the policies of individual institutions and the salaries of particular individuals can be judged. This information is useful where allegations of discrimination are made or where faculty groups demand greater equalization of the structure of salaries. Finally, studies of this type provide useful insights into how the reward structure differs across academic fields. Very few sources of comparative data of this type are available. Yet given the demands for greater equalization of salaries from the faculty unions, it is important to gain a greater understanding of why these differentials exist and how changing them will affect faculty output.

Because both the reward structure and the salary determination process are constantly changing, the cross-section studies discussed in the last chapter, and those that follow, should be interpreted cautiously. Cross-section studies show what is, not what is becoming; that is, the cumulative effects of the set of rules and institutional constraints in each of the years in which the faculty in the sample were in academe. The distinction is an important one, for it suggests that information on the existing reward structure may best be obtained from studies of the determinants of salary changes in the recent past, while data designed to rectify past injustices may best be obtained on a cross-section basis.

Notes

1. David Brown, *The Mobile Professor* (Washington, D. C.: American Council on Education, 1967).

2. For example, the environment at a live-away college gives rise to many forms of learning and pleasure that are by-products of the college experience. Such by-products may affect the demand for the primary goods, but the estimation of their impact goes beyond our present objectives. See Howard P. Tuckman, *The Demand for Higher Education* (Lexington Press: Lexington, Mass., 1972), Chapter 4.

3. The literature in this area is extensive. A good summary may be found in Christopher Jencks, *Inequality: A Reassessment of the Effect of Family and Schooling in America* (New York: Basic Books, 1972), Chapter 7. A more recent example of this type of work appears in Thomas D. Hopkins, "Higher Education Enrollment Demand," *Economic Inquiry* 12 (March 1974): 53-65.

4. An excellent attempt to integrate the enrollment constraint into a model of the educational product market may be found in Arthur Corazzini, Dennis J. Dugan, and Henry G. Grabowski, "Determinants and Distributional Aspects of Enrollment in U.S. Higher Education," *Journal of Human Resources* 7 (Winter 1972): 39-60.

5. In practice, the aggregate adjustment may be reflected in the short run in a shift of students to lower-quality institutions, an increase in the student-faculty ratio, etc. In the longer run, the adjustment is likely to involve the expansion of existing institutions or the development of new ones.

6. An interesting discussion of this point may be found in Larry L. Leslie and Gary P. Johnson, "The Market Model and Higher Education," *Journal of Higher Education* 45 (January 1974): 1-19.

7. At present several theories of learning exist, and a few have been applied in a structured environment. The evidence from these controlled experiments is that no single learning approach appears to be clearly superior. See Edward M. Gramlich and Patricia P. Koshel, *Educational Performance Contracting* (Washington, D.C.: Brookings Institution, 1975), and Alice M. Rivlin and P. Michael Timpane, *Planned Variation in Education* (Washington, D. C.: Brookings Institution, 1975).

8. Of course, the possibility exists that faculty may make greater use of graduate students to perform part of their work.

9. Alternatively, it might be argued that faculty possess these skills in equal measure but fail to cultivate them equally. For a polemic explanation of why this occurs, see Pierre van den Berghe, *Academic Gamesmanship* (New York: Abelard-Schuman, 1970), Chapter 6, and especially p. 73.

10. The same is true of graduate students, who must decide both which areas to specialize in and which skills to develop.

11. The premiums for new faculty are lower than those to established faculty since the latter are more likely to have established specialities. Once a person has chosen to cultivate a particular skill it is difficult for him (her) to change direction,

since time is necessary to make the shift. This introduces short-run rigidities into the marketplace.

12. This helps to explain the importance of outside job offers in creating differentials in faculty salaries.

13. Brown, *College Teachers*, p. 55.

14. Such efforts will have relatively little effect in the aggregate since the talent pool is likely to be limited in the short run.

Discrimination and the Academic Reward Structure

Everyone but an economist knows without asking why money shouldn't buy some things. But an economist has to ask that question. Every asset that lies in the scope of the market is measured by a single yardstick calibrated in dollars. . . . The imperialism of the market's valuation accounts for its contribution, and for its threat to other institutions.

Arthur M. Okun

Federal affirmative action programs, laws passed by several states, and recent court actions have required academic institutions to reevaluate their salary structures. This in turn has forced a rethinking of how equal treatment of faculty can be achieved. Unfortunately, the methods used to equalize salaries by some institutions are not grounded in in a sound theoretical or statistical framework. At least partly as a result, they give rise to salary inequities that may go unrecognized. The purpose of this chapter is to evaluate several proposals for equalizing male and female salaries in terms of the model developed in the last chapter. In the process, evidence will be presented on the existence of differences in the returns to skills for male and female faculty.

Discrimination in Academe

Women faculty have been discriminated against in at least three ways. First, some women have been denied the rights of entry to academic institutions that men have had. Second, women have sometimes received different work assignments than their male colleagues. Third, women have sometimes received a different salary than their male counterparts for performing essentially the same activities with the same skill. Each of these forms of discrimination has affected the welfare of female faculty and all would be eliminated in a nondiscriminating world.

Unfortunately, the outcomes resulting from past discrimination are difficult to distinguish from those resulting from personal choice. If the returns to graduate training are lower for females than for males, fewer females may enter graduate school.[1] Alternatively, women may prefer to enter the labor market or to begin a family after receiving a bachelor's degree. The absence of females in particular graduate programs may reflect past discrimination by employers or women's preference for other activities. It is difficult to infer the cause from the observation that female faculty are underrepresented in academe.

Likewise, female faculty may undertake activities not highly valued by their department, either because it is expected or because they prefer to. If faculty of the opposite sex allocate their time differently among the various activities faculty perform because of different personal preferences, discrimination is difficult to argue; a case may be made for discrimination if their time allocation is different because of decisions by their employers.

A similar problem exists in evaluating differences in the salaries of two faculty members of different sex but equal years of experience. Salary differences may reflect past discrimination against females, perhaps based on the idea that they are secondary breadwinners or that they are tied to their institutions because of their husbands' jobs. Alternatively, these differences may reflect lower productivity for female faculty who take time off for childrearing or who fail to cultivate their skills along lines rewarded by the marketplace. A stronger case can be made for public action where two faculty with equal skills receive different salaries than where the faculty differ in their skill endowments.

What is needed is a yardstick by which equal pay for equally desired and performed work can be assured. A difficulty exists in arriving at such a yardstick. It may be simplistic to assume that two people with similar experience and education are equal in either of the two senses. A reasonable definition of equality should make allowance for differences in skill endowments in establishing both the existence of discrimination in the reward structure and the appropriate remedies.

Equal Salaries for Equal Experience

Several recent proposals for reform of past discrimination practices largely ignore the skill differentials created by the operation of the market. Implicit in these proposals is the view that skill differentials among faculty are either nonexistent or should be eliminated by relating academic salaries to a longevity measure.[2] The primary focus is on equalizing the average salaries of male and female faculty in the same experience and/or education cohort.

A problem with this approach is that current salary differentials reflect, at least in part, demand and supply conditions that existed in the labor market in years past. Past discrimination may have created differential rewards for males and females, either in terms of average salary levels or in terms of the monetary returns to particular skills. Both the method used to rectify the past effects of discrimination and the efficiency and equity effects of this method depend on the pattern that past discrimination has taken.

This point can be seen more clearly by considering several proposals to deal with salary discrimination. One procedure that has gained in popularity recently defines equality between the sexes in aggregate terms. Essentially, a regression equation is used to estimate male salary levels as a function of a limited number of independent variables, usually rank, education, and experience. Each female faculty member is then paid an amount equal to the average salary for a male faculty member of comparable rank, experience, and education level.[3] Such a procedure is simple to understand, easy to administer, and can be implemented with a minimal amount of subjective judgment.

Unfortunately, this method of salary equalization has several problems. Within each experience cohort a distribution of salaries exists, presumably reflecting the effects of the academic labor markets and the reward structure during the years the faculty in this cohort were in academe. This is true for both males and females. Setting *all* female salaries in a given cohort equal to the male *average* eliminates the female distribution but leaves the male distribution unchanged.[4] This has interesting equity implications. Suppose, for example, that prior to the change female faculty with few skills receive lower salaries than females with many skills; the same is true for male faculty. After equalization, no skill differentials will exist for females but a male differential will be preserved. Thus, a new inequity is created.

A numerical example will help to illustrate this point. Three females of high, medium, and low skill levels receive $11,000, $9,000, and $7,000 prior to equalization. Three males of equal experience, education, and skill attainments receive $14,000, $12,000, and $10,000 respectively. To reach equality under this scheme all females in the cohort are given the same salary as the average male. After equalization, they all earn $12,000. The low skill female receives more than her male counterpart, the average female the same, and the high skill female less. Thus, the proposal discriminates in favor of those with few skills and against those with many.

A second difficulty is that differentials in salaries are partially accounted for by differences in the distribution of faculty by field. The salaries of those in the arts and humanities are lower than those in the physical sciences, professions, and biological sciences. Since a higher proportion of females are found in fields offering lower salaries, the average salary of females will be lower than that of males even if both sexes have equal characteristics in other respects. The aggregate salary equalization procedure defined above ignores salary differences due to field. To equalize aggregate female salaries by this approach implies that females in the low-paying fields will earn more than their male counterparts in these fields.

In response to these objections, it should be noted that discrimination may be partially responsible for both the differences in time spent cultivating particular skills by males and females and the unequal distribution of faculty across fields. It may be argued that a procedure that controls for skill and/or field differences perpetuates existing salary differentials between the sexes. However, the effect of equalizing salaries without regard to skill or field differentials is to ignore those decisions made by the market in recognition of prevailing supply and demand conditions. To do so may worsen the condition of female faculty in the long run and work in a direction opposite from the desired one. For example, raising the salaries of females in low-paying fields to the all-field male salary average creates an incentive for more females to enter these fields. This has the effect of equalizing salaries, but it induces more females to enter fields populated primarily by women. If the goal is to create a more equal distribution of female faculty among the academic fields, it may be desirable to allow field-related salary differences to continue to exist. Likewise, if the goal is to allow the market to allocate at least some portion of faculty time among alternative activities, it may be desirable to allow faculty to receive differential salaries according to the skills they possess.

Past discrimination that has taken the form of unequal allocation of work assignments among faculty can be corrected via rules insuring rotation of the less desirable assignments across all faculty, more equal access of female faculty to research time, etc. It seems to be more desirable to attack discrimination at its source than to permit discriminatory practices to continue while masking their operation through equalization of salaries. Where possible, faculty should be free to pursue the activities they desire rather than activities resulting from past discrimination.

Equal Average Salaries

A second proposal for offsetting the past effects of discrimination on female salaries involves raising the mean salary of females to that for males while maintaining the existing distribution of female salaries. This approach differs from the one above in that it takes within-cohort differences as given and simply transfers a lump-sum salary increase to female faculty, the amount determined by the difference between the average salary of females and that of males. Advocates of this approach argue that it is easy to implement, eliminates most of the effects of past discrimination, and effectively merges the separate salary schedules for males and females into a single one.

This is a useful way of dealing with the problem only if employers discriminate against all females equally. Suppose that a female department chairman is paid $2,000 less than a male chairman while a skilled female teacher is paid $500 less than a male teacher. If the mean female salary is $1,000 less than the mean male salary, equalization of average salaries implies that the female department chairman will earn $1,000 less than her male counterpart after equalization while the female teacher will earn $500 more. This outcome, which is similar to the one discussed earlier, involves a particular interpretation of equity; namely, that a just distribution is one that is equal on average.

A similar problem exists if the impact of discriminatory practices differs by field. In those fields where discrimination is minimal or nonexistent, equalization to the male average salary mean creates reverse discrimination against male faculty; in fields where discrimination has created substantial differentials between the sexes, a residually lower salary is given to female faculty.

Equal Pay for Comparable Skills

The best way to equalize salaries appears to be by establishing comparabilities between female and male faculty. Several different methods are available for defining "equals." One way is to identify the individual activities in which faculty engage, assigning a dollar value to each. Equality is then achieved by paying females the same salary as males engaged in the same work. The problem with this method is that it allows for no differences in the quality of work performed; it also requires the identification of an appropriate "reward" for each activity. A variant of this method bases the rewards to faculty on their skills, measured using faculty evaluation reports, outside referees, etc. Such a procedure is time consuming, increases the workload for faculty and administrators, and is inherently subjective.[5]

Some institutions have allowed their female employees to identify a male faculty member with like skills. Salary equality is then achieved by setting the salaries of the paired faculty equal. This approach has the advantage of allowing female faculty to choose their own definition of equality and defend it. But the system is highly subjective, and it depends on the willingness of a faculty member to take an aggressive bargaining stand.[6] For this reason, it is not well suited to aggregate attempts to eliminate discrimination.

A solution favored by the author involves the estimation of the returns to individual attributes through a cross-section regression that includes a suitable set of skill variables. Through this procedure, a set of control variables can be introduced to allow for comparability among faculty. The problem is to identify and construct a reasonable set of skill variables and to establish the existence of a set of market values for the different skills. In the process, it can be determined whether the returns to these skills differ for the two sexes. The sections that follow provide an illustration of such an approach and employ it to examine whether the market provides a comparable return to male and female faculty with equivalent skills.

An Analysis of the Returns to Four Skills

The analysis presented below assumes that faculty potentially possess skills in four areas: teaching, research, public service, and administration. External markets exist for the first three skills, while the market for the last is largely internally generated.[7] A more complete elaboration of faculty skills might include such items as advising and counseling, committee work, and thesis supervision. For present purposes, these additional skills are treated as by-products of the operation of universities and are not separately analyzed. However, they could be incorporated into the analysis with few modifications.

A distinction exists between a faculty member's skills and the activities he or she actually performs. At any point in time what a faculty member does depends, at least in part, on the time available. To make the analysis manageable and to allow for limitations in existing data bases, we shall assume that faculty engage in those activities in which they are skilled and augment their skills by investing time in activities. Where data on skill intensity are not available, evidence that a faculty member is engaged in an activity is taken as a proxy for skill in that activity. Presumably, decisionmakers interested in implementing our approach will replace this assumption with better data on skill intensity.

Several *a priori* judgments can be made about the returns to each of the four skills. The return to good teaching is likely to be the smallest of the measured returns for at least three reasons. First, because everyone in academe is assumed to be able to teach, possession of teaching skills may not differentiate one faculty member from another. Second, because the outputs of an excellent teacher are difficult to define and measure, the market for this type of skill is likely to be ill defined. Third, a teaching reputation is not easily transportable. Because good teaching is usually recognized only locally, few faculty gain a national reputation for teaching.[8]

The market for research skills differs from that for teaching skills. The output of researchers is more visible, consisting of articles, books, and other published pieces which usually reach a national audience. The quality of a researcher's work can be more readily judged by experts, and its worth can be valued in terms of the grants it brings and the reputation of the researcher. Researchers may also be more versatile with quantitative and analytic techniques than are teachers. These arguments would seem to place a relative premium on research skills, which should be reflected in the salary increments received from the publication of articles and books.[9]

Public service entails meeting with communities and public organizations, working on departmental or university committees, and performing charitable or educational activities. Some departments regard these activities highly and demand faculty skilled in them. However, as in the case of teaching, such activities are more likely to receive local than national recognition. The market for faculty with these skills may be limited, given the difficulties inherent in determining a faculty member's public service skills.

Administrative skills are largely learned on the job. Although grant management, departmental and university duties, and prior work experience provide faculty with some skills, much administrative experience is specific to a single institution. Furthermore, administrative skills are not easily measured, and thus the market for this type of skill may be limited. Because administrators have a supervisory role in the department, their salaries are likely to be higher than those of the faculty they supervise.

A faculty member enters the job market possessing more than one skill, and the salary that individual is offered presumably includes a return for each skill valued by the employing department. Thus, it is convenient from an analytic point of view to think of each faculty member as offering a skill package. The salary of each faculty member is at least partially determined by the various quantitities of skills he or she possesses, along with the return each skill commands in the academic markets.

Quantitative Measures of Faculty Skills

The data used in this research were gathered by the American Council on Education (ACE) as part of a 1972-73 national cross-section study of faculty. ACE selected 301 institutions representing diverse institutional types, levels of selectivity, and amounts of institutional wealth. Included are 78 universities, 181 four-year colleges, and 42 junior and community colleges. The original mailing to these schools involved 108,722 individuals; two follow-up mailings, together with the original, produced 53,034 responses. A more complete description of the data may be found elsewhere.[10]

Part-time employees are excluded from the analysis. This is because the determinants of their salaries differ from those of full-time employees. Likewise, the study is confined to faculty at universities. The decision to restrict our focus is based on the realization that the market for individual skills differs by institutional type.[11]

Included in the model are several proxies for faculty skills. Publications serve as a proxy for the skills possessed by researchers. Although it is true that some research does not find its way into the academic journals, the assumption is that faculty valued as researchers are expected to prove their mettle through publication. Journal articles provide proof of a faculty member's ability to conduct research at a level sufficient to meet prevailing standards in his or her discipline. In some fields, books serve the same function.

The number of articles published by a faculty member, measured as of the 1972-73 academic year, is partitioned into six groups (1-2, 3-4, 5-10, 11-20, 21-50, 50+), each represented by a dummy variable that assumes a value of 1 when the number of articles published by the faculty member falls into the corresponding group and 0 otherwise. Books are partitioned into four categories (1-2, 3-4, 5-10, 10+), with a dummy variable assigned to each. The same 0-1 criterion is used. This formulation of the publications variables enables us to examine whether they exert a linear or nonlinear effect on faculty salaries.[12]

An ideal measure of teaching skill would be valid across fields and institutions. One way to acquire such a measure would be to distribute a common student evaluation form to all universities and to use this as a measure of teaching skill. Unfortunately, such a common measure does not currently exist. Some departments do not rate faculty on their teaching quality; those that do follow no common rating scheme. The ACE questionnaire contains information on whether a faculty member has received a teaching award. This is entered as a dummy variable in the regression (1 if yes).

Public service, like teaching, is difficult to quantify. After much debate, a dummy variable denoting whether the faculty member was engaged in unpaid public service (1 if yes) was selected. The implicit assumption is that faculty who are currently engaged in public service have also done so in the past. Thus, evidence of current public service is taken to represent the presence of public-service skills.

Administrative skill is introduced by two dummies. The first assumes a value of 1 if the person lists administration as his or her prime work activity; the second equals 1 if the faculty member was previously a department head or dean.[13] As in the case of public service, these variables measure activity, not intensity.

Other Variables in the Model

Also included in the equation are years of experience, length of time required to complete the highest degree, whether the faculty member has a PhD, several interaction variables between time required to obtain the degree and the PhD and experience variables, and race. Experience, defined as year of highest degree minus year of birth, shows the effect of adding a year to a person's age after the highest degree is received.[14] It is included in the model in a nonlinear form to permit diminishing returns to occur as experience increases. Length of time required to complete the degree (the variable "start" in Table 4-1) is a variable designed to capture the effects of starting an academic career later in life. This represents a variant of the Johnson-Stafford formulation.[15] The PhD variable denotes whether a person has a PhD, LLB, MD, DDS, or EdD. Finally, a dummy variable is included to indicate whether the faculty member is black.

The characteristics of the institution where the faculty member is employed are included with two variables. The first denotes the contractual period of employment (1 if eleven or twelve months); the second is a set of two dummy variables denoting whether the faculty member's department is rated 3.1-4, or 4.1-5 using the Roose-Anderson ratings. The most favorable rating is 5.0, and these variables serve both to measure the effects of being at a quality department and control for article quality. Ideally, we should have liked to control separately for article quality. Unfortunately, the ACE data did not enable us to identify the journals in which faculty publish, and citation data were not available at the time of the study.[16]

Dummy variables are also constructed for the regional location of the

Table 4-1

Determinants of the Variation in Faculty Salaries: All Fields Combined

Variable Name	Male Regression coefficient	Male Cell number	Female Regression coefficent	Female Cell number
Articles				
1-2	$714[a]	1,622[a]	181	258
3-4	882[a]	1,698	1,342[a]	198
5-10	1,467[a]	2,941	1,860	215
11-20	2,325[a]	2,881	3,142[a]	164
21-50	3,766[a]	2,911	5,054[a]	107
50+	6,505[a]	1,622	6,232[a]	32
Books				
1-2	106	4,806	-434	408
3-4	397[c]	2,062	-390	126
5-10	915[a]	1,319	402	73
10+	321	515	-1,126	19
Teaching award	174	2,471	-43	227
Public service	535[a]	7,414	209	704
Current administ.	3,044[a]	2,229	2,345[a]	171
Previous administ.	1,260[a]	4,836	860[b]	305
Experience	550[a]	15,161	386[a]	1,260
Experience squared	-8[a]	15,161	-5[a]	1,260
PhD	2,900[a]	13,766	3,319[a]	979
Time to complete degree (start)	39[b]	15,161	70[c]	1,260
Start x PhD	-40[b]	15,161	-43	1,260
Start x experience	1[d]	15,161	-3[c]	1,260
Black	896	152	3,956[a]	28
Contractual period	3,264[a]	4,973	2,543[a]	417
Department quality rating				
3.1-4.0	824[a]	2,214	-204	141
4.1-5.0	1,048	1,031	76	34
Regions				
North	1,175[a]	3,169	1,725[a]	206
Great Lakes	559[a]	4,442	1,383[a]	363
South	735[a]	2,850	521	218
Field variables				
Professions	1,543[a]	3,260	787[b]	552
Physical science	-1,422[a]	2,547	-1,986[b]	38
Biological sci.	-2,543[a]	1,031	-2,100[a]	78
Liberal arts	-1,278[a]	1,486	-984[b]	178
Math-Engineering	556[a]	2,153	1,096	49
Constant term	6,134[a]	15,161	5,703[a]	1,260
R^2	0.55		0.32	

[a]Coefficient for this variable significant at a 1% confidence level.

[b]Significant at a 5% level.

[c]Significant at a 10% level.

[d]Coefficient less than 1.0.

faculty member's institution (North, Great Lakes, and Southeast) to allow for regional differences in labor markets. A 1 is assigned to the dummy when a department is located in the corresponding region and the Southwest and West are combined in the intercept of the equation.

Because salary levels are in part a function of a faculty member's field, it is important to adjust for field differences. To develop an average reward structure dummy variables are appropriate. However, to the extent that the returns to specific skills differ by fields, an analysis of the reward structure by field calls for a more complex treatment than that developed here.[17] Dummy variables are included for the professions, biosciences, physical sciences, and liberal arts. The social sciences are in the intercept term.[18] The appropriate variable is assigned a 1, depending on the field of the faculty member.

Finally, the salary variable used in the regression consists solely of the income received by a faculty member from his or her employing institution. Excluded are consulting fees, royalties, and other sources of income not derived from the faculty member's educational institution. This is because the focus of our attention is the reward structure at the universities.

The Regression Results

The regression results are shown separately by sex in Table 4-1. The table is read as follows; males with 1-2 articles earn $714 more than those with no articles; those with 3-4 articles earn $882 more. Note that those with no articles or books are included in the intercept. Most of the regression coefficients are for dummy variables, and these are read in the fashion just described. In a few cases, the variables are continuous, and these are read differently. The effect of experience for males is measured by multiplying the number of years of experience by $550 and then subtracting $8 times the square of a faculty member's years of experience. The bottom row of the table shows the amount of the variation in the data explained by the equation (R^2). Appearing in each cell are the number of faculty with the characteristics of that cell. The number in the cells for the continuous variables shows the total faculty in the sample.

What do the results indicate about the rewards to faculty who publish? In both equations, faculty with a large number of publications have a larger salary. Note that the articles increment increases monotonically with articles produced and that each of the variables (with the possible exception of the 1-2 articles for females) is statistically significant. The differences between article categories are appreciable, especially in the 50+ article category. In all cases except the first and last, females earn more for each published article than do their male counterparts.

The salary increments received by authors of books are less dramatic.

Those for males are statistically significant taken as a group, while those for females are not. In neither case is the number of books published related to income. Moreover, the salary increments for book publication are substantially lower than those for article publication. These results suggest that the market places a dollar value on the number of publications a faculty member produces. But as we shall show in the next chapter, both the likelihood of receiving an increment and the size of the increment depend on the faculty member's field.

Before leaving the publication variables, it is important to note the decline in the 10+ books category. Examination of the zero-order correlation coefficients between this variable and the other independent variables suggests that multicollinearity is not a factor accounting for the decline. One explanation for these results is that faculty who publish more than ten books find the time to do this by reducing their participation in other activities. Since their rewards are likely to be external ones excluded by our salary measure, their efforts appear to produce a negative reward. Inclusion of their outside income from royalties might thus alter this conclusion. An alternative explanation is that the model contains no control for the quality of the books produced. Publishers of ten or more books may concentrate on updating their textbooks or edited works. Presumably, these are not highly valued by academic departments.

Males who have received an outstanding teaching award average $174 more than their unrewarded peers. This amount, which is less than 15% of the salary increment of males with 1-2 articles, does not differ in a statistical sense from no increment.[19] Females also do not receive a statistically significant salary increment for outstanding teaching. These results seem to suggest that outstanding teaching, at least as measured here, goes unrecognized.

Given the nature of our measure, this may be too strong a conclusion, however. For one thing, some institutions do not offer teaching awards. In these institutions, good teachers may receive a salary increment but since their teaching ability is not recognized by our measure, there would be no record that their efforts were rewarded. Further, without a measure of teaching ability that allows for differences in effort, the meaning of this variable is difficult to decipher. Despite these objections to our measure, it is not clear that a better alternative is available unless several measures of teaching skills are used. The effects of good teaching are not easy to capture, and this may well be a factor determining the rewards to the teaching skill.

Public service is recognized by a larger salary increment, on the average, than is teaching. Males earn an average $535 more if they engage in this activity. In contrast, females earn an average $209 more, but this amount is not statistically significant. The increment to administration is substantial, especially for males. Current administrators earn $3,044 more if they are males and $2,345 if they are females. Both amounts are statistically significant.

The Existence of Skill Differentials by Sex

Our findings present quantitative evidence of the existence of statistically significant differences in the returns to the four skills among male and female faculty. Apparently, female faculty who have published a number of articles equivalent to those of their male counterparts receive a higher salary increment on the average for publication. This may be due to the fact that fewer females than males publish. If so, a sudden burst of publications from females could wipe out the observed differential. Alternatively, it might reflect some other characteristic of females who publish; for example, continuity of stay in the labor force.[20] While we cannot infer an explicit cause from the data, it is provocative to note that the publication skill is the only one in which females appear to earn more than their male colleagues, at least over a large publication interval. This may provide a useful insight into the reward structure for those females wondering how to succeed in academe.

In contrast, females with an equivalent number of books to males earn less of a salary increment. Outstanding teaching is not rewarded in any meaningful sense for either sex, and public service and administration yield higher returns to male faculty than to females.

The explanation for these differentials is complex and probably relates to the existence of different sets of rules and markets for the two sexes. But what the results imply is that aggregate policies for redress that do not recognize skill comparabilities will create inequities between males and females with similar skills. They are also unlikely to eliminate the differential returns to the individual skills created by the operation of a dual system of rewards.

On the other hand, a policy designed to pay females an experience increment equal to their male equivalents will have a considerable impact on female salaries, even after control variables are introduced to allow for skill differences. This may be illustrated by computing an average salary for males and females from the regression coefficients in Table 4-1, using different entry dates and years of experience to see how female salaries fare relative to those of males. The results, presented in Table 4-2, are based on the average salaries of male and female faculty with a PhD, no publications, no teaching awards, and no public service or administrative service. The calculation is for a white social scientist employed on a nine-month basis in a Western department with a quality rating less than 3.

The figures in Table 4-2 suggest that females earn a starting salary at least $500 more than males with equivalent backgrounds. This is likely to be a reflection of the more attractive labor market conditions for young females resulting from affirmative action programs. As years of experience increase, female salaries fall behind those of males. A policy that sets female salaries equal to the average male salaries at their experience level would have a substantial effect on the average level of female salaries, especially for those with

Table 4-2
Salaries for Comparable Male and Female Faculty by Starting Age and
Experience Level

Age at Time of Completion of Highest Degree	Years of Experience				
	1	10	20	30	35
Male					
27	$ 9,546	$13,607	$16,595	$17,977	$18,067
30	9,542	13,593	16,569	17,941	18,024
35	9,537	13,570	16,527	17,879	17,953
Female					
27	$10,057	$12,325	$13,879	$14,415	$14,301
30	10,129	12,320	13,788	14,237	14,081
35	10,250	12,312	13,636	13,942	13,714
Female salary as a percentage of male salary					
27	105%	91%	84%	80%	79%
30	106	91	83	79	78
35	107	91	83	78	76

Note: Computed from Table 4-1 coefficients carried to four decimal places. For assumptions behind the computations, see text.

many years of experience. The salary of the average female who began her career at age 30 and had twenty years of experience would rise by $2,781; for those with thirty years of experience, it would rise by $3,704.

Implications for Salary Equalization Schemes

Since a number of control variables are entered into the regression to account for differences in both the skill endowments and the distribution of male and female faculty, it is tempting to attribute the lower return to females to past discrimination. Unfortunately, it cannot be established that the variables chosen for the regression adequately control for differences in the quality of effort for the two sexes. It may be that female publishers write better articles or men make better administrators. A conclusive claim of discrimination based on our crude data does not seem to be justified.

The findings are suggestive, however. It is difficult to explain, for example, why female administrators are paid less than their male counterparts or why the returns to experience are lower for females even after so many different factors are controlled.[21] It is also interesting to note that the R^2s for the two equations shown in Table 4-1 differ considerably. The male equation explains a reasonably large amount of the variation in male salaries (0.55); the amount of variation in female salaries explained by the female equation is a good deal smaller (0.32).

These results may imply that female salaries are more random than male salaries or, alternatively, that they are subject to influences other than those described here: Among the more obvious ones are husband's occupation, time spent out of the labor force in childrearing, and field of specialization. Whether these factors should affect female salaries is a separate question that no regression equation can answer; whether they are the cause of the differences shown here remains to be established. What is clear on the basis of our data is that the evidence suggests that the distribution of salaries is not the same for the two sexes.

Taken in total, the findings in this chapter indicate that the market does appear to reward skill differences among faculty. On this basis, further efforts to quantify these differences among faculty seem warranted. The data also suggest that similar rewards are not received by males and females engaged in similar activities. Thus, aggregate attempts to equalize salaries which do not recognize skill differentials create new forms of inequities among faculty. In the next chapter we analyze the reward structure further by examining the question of how salaries differ by field. In the process, we also explore the question of how a common reward structure such as that proposed by several unions would affect existing incentives.

Notes

1. The future returns to graduate training are determined both by nonacademic employers and by the educational institutions that hire persons with graduate degrees. Past discrimination in academe can affect the current number of females entering graduate school through the effects this has had on expected financial returns.

2. The idea that salary should be related to years in the labor force is a common one that finds widespread support among people with different views of what an equitable salary distribution ought to look like. Issues arise, however, when it is recognized that at any experience level salaries are distributed unequally. The problem becomes one of defining what the ideal within-cohort distribution ought to be.

3. An example of this approach is presented in a recent paper by Robert E. Wall entitled "Salary Inequities: Identification and Adjustment," presented at the American Educational Research Association Meetings in April 1976.

4. An alternative proposal corrects only those female salaries that deviate substantially from those of males. The same objections apply to this approach as are given below, since such a procedure may create new inequities.

5. The limitations of these evaluations are well known. See, for example, Alan Kelley, "Uses and Abuses of Course Evaluations as Measures of Education Output," *Journal of Economic Education* 4 (Fall 1972).

6. If females have lower self-concepts than males, for example, they may underestimate their true abilities and thus not achieve salary equality. Alternatively, a female who engages in strategic behavior will find it useful to choose a well-paid faculty member as her point of comparison.

7. It seems reasonable to distinguish separately the market for administrators for several reasons. First, the process governing administrators' salaries is further removed from the market for educational services than is the process governing the salaries of teachers and researchers. Second, educational institutions have considerable say over both the type of administrative skills they need and the ratio of administrators to faculty. Third, skill acquisition by administrators is largely a learning-by-doing process. In contrast, possibilities exist for skill acquisition through course work by researchers and teachers.

8. David G. Brown, *The Market for College Teachers: An Economic Analysis of Career Patterns among Southeastern Social Scientists* (Durham: University of North Carolina Press, 1965), pp. 203-06.

9. Grant and contract procurements may bring their own rewards. However, we assume that they are intermediate outputs of the research production process, the outcome of which is scholarly publication.

10. Alan E. Bayer, *Teaching Faculty in Academe: 1972-73* (Washington, D.C.: American Council on Education, 1973).

11. Extensive analyses of the data revealed that a better-developed reward structure exists at universities than at two- and four-year colleges. A more comprehensive set of skill variables than were available from the ACE data source is needed to explain the divergent patterns that are found in the latter institutions. Concentration on university rewards should not be taken to mean that the reward structure for other institutions is less interesting, only that it is more difficult to identify.

12. The returns to each additional publication diminish as the number of publications produced increases. This point is examined further in Chapter 6.

13. A person no longer in an administrative position is assumed to experience an erosion of skills. At the same time, the salary increment to past administration is preserved in that person's salary. To capture this effect, we add the second dummy variable for administration.

14. This specification of experience is a common one in the literature. However, it implicitly assumes that faculty take no time off in pursuing their academic careers and that all time spent after obtaining the highest degree yields experience of benefit in academe.

15. George E. Johnson and Frank P. Stafford, "Lifetime Earnings in a

Professional Labor Market: Academic Economists," *Journal of Political Economy* 82 (May/June 1974): 549-569.

16. Since the quality rating of a department depends in part on the quality of the articles published by its faculty, inclusion of this variable may provide a partial control for article quality. However, significant differences in article quality often exist within a single department. Problems also exist in providing for differences in articles due to their length, whether they are jointly authored, and the frequency of their citation. See Alan E. Bayer and John Folger, "Some Correlates of a Citation Measure of Productivity in Science," *Sociology of Education* 39 (Fall 1966): 381-91.

17. This point is explored in greater detail in Chapter 5, where data for the individual fields are presented.

18. The five disciplines are grouped on the basis of the HEGIS taxonomy. The variables include the following fields: *social science*—anthropology, geography, economics, history, political science, psychology, and sociology; *liberal arts*—english, music; *math-engineering*—civil and electrical engineering, mathematics; *biological sciences*—biochemistry, botany, zoology; *physical sciences*—chemistry, earth sciences, physics; *professions*—education, law, medicine, pharmacy. These fields were selected on the basis of their representativeness of the broader data available in the ACE study and to economize on the cost of including all of the over seventy fields in the regression.

19. No hard-and-fast rules exist on what is an acceptable significance level to apply. Normally, the 0.01 and 0.05 levels of significance are used. Given the large number of observations in the regression and our unwillingness to reject a coefficient when it is correct, we have chosen a 0.05 level for the significance test. However, both the 0.01 and the 0.10 values are given in Table 4-1 to enable the reader to make his own judgments.

20. For two different views on this issue, see George E. Johnson and Frank P. Stafford, "The Earnings and Promotion of Women Faculty," *American Economic Review* 64 (December 1974): 901-03, and Marianne A. Ferber, "Professors, Performance, and Rewards," *Industrial Relations* 13 (February 1974): 76.

21. Presumably, the experience variable measures the effect of longevity after the skills valued in the marketplace are removed. However, it is also likely to contain any skills not included in the regression, cohort effects, and the effects of measurement error in the four skill variables that are included. Even if allowance is made for the presence of these omitted variables in the experience variable, the substantial relative decline in female salaries is difficult to explain other than by reference to the past discriminatory practices of employers.

Aggregate versus Field-Related Rewards

The specialist can do everything, or he will soon be able to do so. All are specialists in their little realms, and they expect to get what they require from other specialists. All of them live as if the whole were being directed from a single place. . . . The one truth exists in the contest of authorities that are joined together by the fact that first of all they meet in the common medium of scientific attitudes and secondly their authentic selves are of concern to one another, are in search of one another, and pay heed to one another.

K. Jasper

Several reasons exist for examining the reward structure of the individual academic fields. To the extent that the salary structure of the various fields differs, aggregate schemes which attempt to remedy discrimination by raising female salaries to the male average are likely to have undesirable effects for female faculty in some fields. Moreover, attempts to impose a single salary schedule for all faculty, resulting either from legislative fiat or union demands, will also have unanticipated effects both of an efficiency and of an equity nature. Finally, if different structures exist, the allocation of faculty time among alternative activities is likely to differ across fields. Imposition of a common salary schedule on faculty will change the incentive structure across fields and this may have an effect on how faculty allocate their time at the margin. These are important issues and we shall devote the bulk of this chapter to exploring their implications.

Systematic Examination of Differences in the Reward Structure by Field

Existing studies of the structure of academic salaries typically employ dummy variables to control for individual field differences, following the approach pursued in the last chapter.[1] This procedure has several advantages. It is economical, permitting researchers to analyze the salary structure of a number of different fields with comparatively few variables. It provides a partial control for changes in the distribution of faculty by field, and it enables researchers to capture the average salary increments to individual skills, using a regression procedure. This can be quite useful for those occasions when one wishes to obtain data on the average or marginal increment to salary resulting from the exercise of a particular skill. It is also helpful in describing the characteristics of the "typical faculty member."

The dummy variable approach applied in the last chapter does not permit a test of the hypothesis that the returns to individual skills differ across fields. The economist, biologist, chemist, and internist are all assumed to receive the same salary increment for their teaching, publication, public service, and administrative skills. This may be an acceptable assumption when the goal is to derive an average return to faculty for teaching or research. It may also be useful in describing the average career path or earnings-experience profiles of faculty. But, if the returns to the individual skills differ by field, this approach gives rise to the misleading impression that a particular policy or set of policies designed to standardize faculty salaries will have an equal effect on faculty in all fields. As a result, important equity issues may be ignored.

Compelling reasons exist for believing that both the structure of salaries, and the rewards faculty receive differ by field. Consider for example the demand for different courses. Presumably, the demand for a single course, or a set of courses, is related to student preferences. An increase in business majors may raise student-teacher ratios in the business school in the short run and the demand for faculty to teach these courses in the longer run. Course requirements set down by the college, tenure restrictions, and other factors make the link between the demand for courses and their supply a weak one. But the existence of this link gives rise to the possibility that market forces can create differential rewards by field. If supply factors also differ, salary differences are likely to arise.

On the supply side, relatively few opportunities exist for movement of faculty across fields. An occasional person may switch fields, but there is little evidence to suggest that substantial numbers of faculty shift their interests in response to changes in relative supply and demand. The body of knowledge that characterizes most academic fields requires time to acquire. A further barrier to movement is the requirement of a PhD or other advanced degree in the field in which the faculty member wishes to teach. Psychological and emotional factors also operate to discourage shifting.

On balance, both supply and demand arguments suggest that salary differentials may be market related. But a number of nonmarket impediments may potentially offset the operation of these market forces. For example, the administration of a particular university may mandate that all of its faculty should receive equal percentage dollar increases. This has the effect of widening the distribution of salaries. Alternatively, a common salary schedule may be imposed on a university by its board of trustees, board of regents, or faculty union. Such a schedule imposes a set of salary increments related to experience and rank which make no allowance for cross-field differences. In the absence of a single national salary schedule, actions effective at particular institutions are unlikely to eliminate cross-field salary differences in national labor markets. Those whose field commands a return higher than that provided by the common-schedule institution will be bid away to another institution that offers a higher return. Those in fields that command a lower return elsewhere will remain at their present institutions.[2] We shall return to this point shortly. For the present, it is sufficient to note that the presence of a single salary schedule at some institutions does not preclude salary differences by field at the national level.

The intensity and nature of the skills faculty possess may differ by field. Some fields (i.e., art) may require relatively little preclass instruction but relatively large in-class faculty-student interaction; others (i.e., a graduate course in economic theory) may involve intensive preclass preparation but relatively little in-class interaction. If the academic reward structure recognizes differences in teaching skills of either type, the returns to the teaching skill need not be the same in the two fields. Alternatively, if the time required to develop a skill differs by field, differential returns to the individual skills may emerge.

The importance of differences in both supply and demand in affecting the returns to the individual skills by field can be illustrated using the publication skill. In some of the biological sciences, innovative research involves a heavy investment in conceptualization and experimental design. Length of publication is not a critical factor in determining the acceptability of a piece of research to a journal and neither is familiarity with a large body of research. As a result, if an experiment is successful, one can usually expect a number of articles to flow from it. In contrast, in a field like political science, publication may involve large amounts of data collection, substantial familiarity with the literature, and/or an ability to integrate present research with the conceptual work of others. Lead time for publication is often long, and as a result the average number of publications by a faculty member in political science may be more limited than in the biological sciences. Because differences in the conditions for the supply of articles may give rise to different returns to publication, an argument can be made at the conceptual level for differential returns to the research skill by field.[3]

Differences in the average level of faculty salaries across fields may also relate to the differential opportunities for alternative employment available to faculty. The skills cultivated by academicians in different fields are not equally marketable in the nonacademic world. Medieval literature scholars, French historians, and other specialized scholars may find it difficult to find a job that allows the use of their skills outside academe. To the extent that the amount of labor offered by this group is less responsive to salary changes than the labor supply of more mobile faculty (i.e., business school, legal, medical, or economics faculty), it might be expected that salary differentials will emerge between the two groups.

Essentially the same argument can be made for differences in the skill endowments of faculty. While some persons may take the view that all of the faculty in a mobile field are more mobile than their counterparts in a less

mobile field, this need not be the case in reality. Some professors of English
have better employment opportunities than some economists; some historians
more opportunities than some professors of law. However, to the extent that
some skills make a faculty member more marketable than others, and to the
extent that nonacademic opportunities differ by discipline, the returns to alternative skill endowments may differ by field.

Finally, differential returns may exist because the basic decisions made by
departments reflect different professional values placed on faculty skills.[4] Departments generally have considerable say over who is hired and how salary
increments are distributed. Given the substantial amount of crossfertilization
within each profession and the desire of most department members to gain
some measure of recognition from their peers the departments have an incentive
to develop a reward structure resembling that of the larger profession to which
they belong. Within the constraints imposed by the institutional setting, these
pressures are likely to lead to the creation of a field-related salary structure.

In Favor of a Common Salary Structure

In light of the above arguments, it seems useful to examine the rationale for
applying a single salary structure to all faculty. Three arguments are usually
advanced in support of this approach. The first involves the need to eliminate
the vestiges of past discrimination along the lines advanced in the last chapter.
The second argues the need for a more well defined and simplified salary structure. The third concerns the need for creating a more equitable salary structure.

Proponents of the first argument note that many fields traditionally favored
by females have average faculty salaries lower than the all-field average. This is
especially true for home economics and nursing, but it also applies to the fields
of education and social welfare. A salary structure that allows cross-field differences implicitly sanctions male-female differentials and thus insures that
female faculty will continue to earn less than males. If the goal is to eliminate
salary differences between the sexes, and if the existing distribution of faculty
is to be preserved, an aggregate salary structure that makes no allowances for
field seems to be warranted.

The problem with this argument is that while it is highly desirable to eliminate discrimination against women in academe, it is not clear that equalization
of salaries across fields should be justified on this basis. Females in graduate
school are free, subject to past socializing influences, to choose among alternative graduate studies. When they are not, means are available to insure their
free choice of a graduate field. If more women than men *voluntarily* choose a
lower-paying field of study over a higher one, differences in the nonpecuniary
preferences of the sexes are likely to be involved.

An increase in the salaries of females in the low-paid fields to a level based on the male all-field average will raise the combined monetary and nonmonetary returns to females in female-favored fields relative to those of females in traditionally male-favored fields. Other things being equal, this induces more women to seek graduate training in traditionally female fields. Salaries are equalized but the distribution of female faculty across fields may become even more unequal. This outcome may be acceptable if the goal of social policy is solely to achieve financial equality for females. But several feminist groups, and many of those concerned with discrimination in academe, have expressed concern about the underrepresentation of women in some academic fields. To the extent that equality of distribution is a desirable goal along with that of salary equality, the single salary structure solution may not be a satisfactory one.[5]

A further problem exists if a single salary structure is applied at a single institution with a fixed amount of money for faculty compensation. In this instance, mobile faculty who face a cut relative to the higher salaries they would have received without the single salary schedule are likely to move to another institution. These are likely to be the faculty with skills most valued by the marketplace. Those with skill endowments equal to or less than those available on the national market would remain at the institution in the short run.

On balance, some downgrading of skills will occur at that institution. How much of a downgrading will probably depend on the size of the differential paid to the different skills in that institution relative to the national market, and on the tightness of academic labor markets. In the longer run, the effect on the average skill level of the institution will probably be somewhat greater as faculty who are unhappy upgrade their skills and leave, give up and allow their skills to become obsolete, or enter the institution with fewer skill endowments.

Some skilled females may be gainers under this proposal, and these persons may stay at their home institution. This would be the case if past discrimination kept their salaries lower than the male average. But for the reasons described in the last chapter, these females may not receive as high a return to their skills as would be possible under a proposal recognizing true comparability of skills. As a result, fewer women would be expected to increase their investment in skills than under the comparability approach suggested in the last chapter.

A single salary structure is substantially easier to administer than the present salary structure. It involves less time spent in making salary decisions, eliminates some of the subjectivity of the existing process, and enables faculty to look toward the future with greater certainty about their future returns. If such a structure can be implemented along with a substantial salary increase for all faculty, even highly skilled faculty may gain in the process. Whether skills will be improved as a result will then depend on whether income or substitution effects are predominant.[6] However, the single salary schedule will be less efficient than a market-determined one in the sense that faculty in fields paying below-average salaries will receive a salary higher than that needed to keep them in academe.[7] Whether a single salary schedule insuring net gains to all faculty can be implemented is a political question involving a judgment about the relative priority that education should receive.

A single national salary schedule imposed on all faculty, for example through the creation of a national bargaining union, would have many of the adverse effects described earlier. Faculty would no longer be free to move among schools to raise their salaries, but they could leave academe if they wished to do so. Those with skills useful in nonacademic jobs would have an incentive to leave academe; others might allow their skills to become obsolete.[8] Unskilled faculty would probably be net gainers. How significant the effects would be on the quality of work effort put forth by faculty would depend on whether national bargaining made it possible for faculty to make a financial gain relative to persons with comparable skills outside academe. It would also depend on the return allowed for the development of individual skills.

The equity argument is difficult to evaluate with any degree of rigor. To the extent that faculty are members of the same institution, put in similar hours, and work equally hard, a reasonable argument can be made for a salary structure that rewards them equally. To the extent that faculty expend unequal amounts of effort, the argument rests largely on aesthetic considerations. However, if salaries are currently based on arbitrary criteria, a single salary structure might be justified on the grounds that this creates a more just system of reward than the current one. Such a schedule may also unify faculty by eliminating individual bargaining in favor of a common bargaining goal. But unless the bargaining covers a substantial majority of faculty, limits will exist to the ability of the single schedule institutions to eliminate field differences in the national labor markets.

Whether one favors a single salary structure, a system based on a common base salary but with differential rewards to skills, or the preservation of the status quo, depends on the relative weight given to the equity and efficiency arguments presented above. The tradeoff between the two goals is a familiar one to economists and to others concerned with the economic effects of alternative programs.

While no simple solution exists to bring harmony between the two competing goals, it is helpful to determine that a conflict between the two exists. In the last chapter, we established that field-related differences in the average salaries of faculty exist even after controls are introduced for differences in skill endowments and other characteristics. We shall now examine the returns to different skills in several select academic fields to see if they differ. A finding that they do suggests that the efficiency arguments presented above may be important; a finding that the returns to the individual skills are similar across fields may imply that the arguments are more conceptual than real.

Do the Returns to Faculty Skills Differ by Field?

In order to explore this question with some degree of rigor, the model introduced in the last chapter is estimated separately for faculty in each of the fields in our sample. The same model is used to estimate the returns to the four skills in each field, even though different variables might be employed to explain the variance of a music faculty member's salary than to explain the variance of a medical school faculty member's salary. This insures that a comparable set of skills are examined, but it leaves open the possibility that the wrong skills are measured. Since our goal is to examine both whether and how the returns to four commonly defined sets of skills differ by field, we shall accept the possibility of misspecification bias. But it seems reasonable to assume that different results might be obtained than those developed here if a model designed to maximize the amount of explained variance was estimated separately for each field.

A further simplification is introduced for the reader's convenience. To avoid the presentation of a massive number of tables, the results for the individual field regressions are not presented in tabular form. Since both the form of the model and a discussion of the variables it employs have already been presented in Chapter 4, only the regression coefficients and the significance levels for the four skill variables are presented in the discussion that follows.

Because the number of females in our sample is not sufficiently large to permit separate equations to be estimated, we are unable to identify the existence of differential returns by field for this group. The results for males suggest differential returns to the four skills by field, and since our preliminary results suggest that, for all faculty combined, females earn less than males in three out of the four skills, it is not improbable to suggest that females will receive a differentially lower return for their skills than males. Evidence of this phenomenon may be found in a separate paper examining discrimination in the social sciences.[9]

Social Sciences

The social sciences included in our study are anthropology, economics, geography, history, political science, and sociology. In economics, geography, and sociology, article publication is an important determinant of salaries, and those with a large number of articles receive substantially more than those with no articles. A faculty member in economics with 1-2 articles earns $1,106 more than one with no articles; in geography and sociology, the salary increment does not differ significantly from zero. A faculty member with over fifty articles earns $6,767 more than one with no articles in economics, $3,258 more in geography, and $7,033 in sociology. In anthropology, the link between articles published and salary is neither systematic nor statistically significant.

In history, those with over fifty articles earn $3,217 more than those with no articles, but the salary increments below this publication level display no systematic pattern. Political scientists with 11-20 or 21-50 articles receive statistically significant returns ($1,301 and $3,010 respectively), but the link between articles published and salary is tenuous in the other categories. Likewise, in psychology, substantial and statistically significant increments of $2,287 and $4,186 are observed in the 21-50 and 50+ categories.

The proportion of faculty with no articles varies by field. In psychology it is 3%, in anthropology and geography 7%, in sociology 8%, in economics 11%, and in history and political science 13%. The median number of articles produced by a faculty member is 5-10 in all of the social sciences except psychology (median 11-20 articles).

Book publishers receive large, statistically significant, and monotonically rising salary increments in economics and psychology. In history, political science, and sociology, the relationship between book publication and salary is disturbed by a downturn in the last category similar to that observed in Table 4-1. Book publication does not have a statistically significant effect on salaries in anthropology and has an uneven effect in geography. In all of the fields, the returns to article publication are greater than the returns to book publication.

Outstanding teaching brings a statistically significant salary increment only in geography ($1,060). (In history, the increment of $616 is significant only at a 10% level which we have ruled unacceptable for current purposes.) Public service is rewarded in economics ($541), history ($1,110), political science ($789), and sociology ($922).

In contrast, with the exception of anthropology, current administration brings a statistically significant salary increment in all fields. For economics, it is $3,987, for geography $3,063, for history $5,314, for political science $3,927, for psychology $2,497, and for sociology $2,045. Previous administration brings an increment of $1,521, $848 (significant at a 10% level), $1,361, $1,211, $1,353, and $1,291 for each field respectively.

Engineering and Mathematics

Article publication brings a significant salary increment in all three fields in this category. With minor exceptions, the progression is monotonically upward, and in all cases it is statistically significant. In civil engineering, those with 1-2 articles earn $1,188 more than those with no articles, and those with over 50 articles earn $6,312 more. In electrical engineering, the comparable amounts are $284 and $4,940, and in mathematics they are $1,417 and $6,936 respectively. In all three fields, the median number of articles is 5-10 but the median is closer to 11-20 in mathematics.

Book publication has a nonsystematic effect on salaries. In civil engineering, it has no effect; in electrical engineering its effect is significant in the 3-4 and 5-10 book intervals. In mathematics, it is significant only in the 1-2 and 3-4 book ranges.

Outstanding teaching is not rewarded in any of the three fields. Public service raises a faculty member's average salary by $1,215 in civil engineering and $576 in mathematics; it is not significant in electrical engineering. Current administration raises average salary by $2,563 in civil engineering, $2,945 in electrical engineering, and $2,440 in mathematics. The amounts for past administration are respectively $1,917, $2,923, and $1,567.

Physical Sciences

Article publication is not directly related to salaries in chemistry and earth sciences except in the 50+ category. With one exception, salaries rise with the number of articles published in physics, but the increments are small until the 21-50 category. In all three fields, over 98% of the faculty have published at least one article. For those who have published over 50 articles, the salary increments relative to nonpublishers are $4,955 in chemistry, $4,855 in earth science, and $7,764 in physics.

The median number of articles for the three fields respectively is 21-50, 11-20 and 11-20 (approaching 21-50). These medians are substantially larger than those presented earlier. The difference may be explainable by the supply arguments presented earlier in the chapter.

Book publication has a monotonically increasing and statistically significant effect on salaries in chemistry. A person with over 10 books averages $2,300 more than his nonpublishing counterpart. In contrast, a significant effect of book publication on salaries is observed in earth sciences only for those with 5-10 books, and in physics only for those with 1-2 books. Outstanding teaching brings a statistically significant negative reward in earth science (−$1,057), while public service is positively rewarded in chemistry ($486) and physics ($1,070).

Current administration is rewarded in all fields, though by differential amounts. In chemistry, the increment is $2,557, in earth science $5,179, and in physics $3,326. The rewards to past administration are respectively $1,970, $1,816, and $2,265.

Liberal Arts

English and music are the two fields chosen to represent the liberal and fine arts. In English, the relation between articles published and salary is a monotonically increasing one, and increments beyond the first are statistically significant. A faculty member with 5-10 articles averages $1,161 more per year than one with no articles; one with over 50 articles earns $5,556 more. In music, the pattern is uneven, and statistically significant increments are observed only in the 11-20 and 21-50 article categories ($1,821 and $2,445 respectively). The median number of articles published is 5-10 in English and 1-2 in music. But over 36% of the music faculty in our sample reported no published articles.[10]

The relationship between books published and salary is a monotonically increasing and statistically significant one for all the intervals except the first in English. A faculty member with over 10 books receives $3,419 more than a non-book publisher. In contrast, a statistically significant salary increment exists for those with over 10 books in music (increment $1,091). Outstanding teaching is rewarded in neither field, and public service is rewarded only in music ($645).

Substantial differences in rewards also exist for administrators. Those currently in administration receive a salary increment of $2,216 in English and $4,074 in music. Those previously in administration earn $2,974 in English and $1,688 in music.[11] The large salary increment to musician administrators may reflect the fact that musician's salaries are traditionally lower than the faculty average while administrator's salaries are traditionally higher. A musician named to a universitywide post may thus require a larger than average salary increment in order to achieve a salary even roughly comparable to that of other college administrators.

The Professions

Four fields are included in the analysis of the professions: education, law, medicine, and pharmacy. The results suggest that the former two categories are similar to each other and different from the last two categories. In education, a faculty member publishing 1-2 articles averages $877 more than someone with no articles; a law faculty member averages $2,290 more. The salary structures of both professions exhibit monotonically increasing dollar returns to article publication. A faculty member with over 50 articles earns $4,565 more than the nonpublisher in education; in law the figure is $5,407.[12] In contrast, article publishers earn negative but nonsignificant returns over a broad interval in medicine and pharmacy. This surprising finding appears to be related to two things: differences in the relative supply of articles and the structural determinants of medical and pharmacy faculty salaries.[13]

The median number of articles published in both law and education is 5-10 and roughly 15% of the faculty in each field have published 21 or more articles. In contrast, over 97% of those in medicine and 99% of those in pharmacy have published. The median for both fields is 21-50 articles.

The relative ease of publication for medical and pharmacy faculty may explain the low returns well-published faculty receive. But the low R^2 on the regression for medical faculty (0.24) warrants further explanation. Medical salaries are affected by several factors that our model does not capture. These include the duties performed by faculty members, the quality and affluence of their departments, and their field of specialization. The salaries of faculty members in medical schools relate to their patient load, courses taught, administrative responsibilities, and research interests.[14] Quality of department seems to be a reasonable proxy for departmental wealth, particularly in the form of external grant and contract support.[15] In terms of the conceptual scheme developed in Chapter 3, this wealth permits less reliance on traditional markets in determining salary levels.

Field of specialization is also an important variable in explaining the variation in salaries in medical schools. A recent study by the Association of American Medical Colleges suggests that among full-time full professors employed in clinical science departments, mean salaries ranged from $33,200 for those in preventive medicine to $55,300 for plastic surgeons.[16] The range is even greater when faculty with nonmedical degrees are included. Since the variation in salaries is considerably greater in medicine than in the other fields reported in this study, it is not surprising that a more complex model is needed to explain the salaries of medical faculty.

Book publication has a monotonically increasing effect on salaries only in the field of education. In this field, a faculty member with over 10 books averages $1,311 more than one with no books. In all of the other fields, the coefficients are largely random and not statistically significant.

The teaching variable is not statistically significant in any of the regressions. This is a somewhat surprising finding for the field of education since one might hope that at least in this field a good teaching job would be recognized. One explanation for this finding may be that our measure of teaching skill is a weak one. But the lack of a meaningful relationship between salary and teaching provides food for thought. A more complete analysis of the education regression can be found elsewhere.[17]

Public service is statistically significant only in education ($628). In three fields, current administration is rewarded: education ($2,670), law ($3,944), and medicine ($4,278). Past administration has a statistically significant effect on salaries only in education ($1,562) and medicine ($3,025).

Biological Sciences

A systematic relationship between articles published and salaries does not exist in any of the three fields included in this category. Although a faculty member with over 50 articles earns $5,240 more than a nonpublisher in biochemistry, $3,328 more in botany, and $3,751 more in zoology (significant at a 10% level), the returns to those with fewer articles are not statistically significant. This may again relate to relative supply considerations. Virtually all of the biochemists in the sample have published. The comparable percentages are 98% for botany and 99% for zoology. The medians for the three fields are 5-10, 11-20, and

21-50, and the size of the regression coefficients, together with the sign of these coefficients appears to be related to where these medians fall.[18]

Book publication has no statistically significant effect on salaries in any of the three fields, although the 3-4 book interval is significant in biochemistry ($1,569). Outstanding teaching is associated with a statistically significant salary increment only in botany ($1,472), while public service has no significant effect on salaries. In all three fields current administration results in a large salary increment: $4,598 in biochemistry, $4,497 in botany, and $2,673 in zoology. Previous administration has a $2,516 effect on salary in biochemistry and a $1,624 effect in zoology.

Implications

The returns to the individual skills appear to differ by field, in some cases substantially. This is not surprising since the skills required of faculty also differ by field. Musicians' salaries are affected to some extent by the number of performances they give, artists' by their number of showings in art galleries, physical scientists' by the success of their experiments. Educators are evaluated in part on their public service, while in medicine public service may be measured in terms of patient load. Brown's argument that no single labor market exists for faculty takes on considerable meaning in this context.

Despite the wide divergence in skill requirements by field, the conceptual framework developed in this chapter serves a useful analytic purpose. What it shows is that a rational system of direct salary rewards exists in academe and that it can be quantified in a fairly formalistic manner.

The major insights offered by this chapter appear to be the following: first, those who publish articles are likely to receive a higher salary than those who do not, although in those fields where an overwhelming majority of faculty publish, primarily the biological, medical, and physical sciences, article publication brings a substantial increment to salary only for those with very large numbers of publications. While we have offered an explanation for this in terms of relative supply arguments, the reasons for this phenomenon remained to be established. Second, those with outstanding teaching awards seldom receive a salary increment in recognition of their skills; when they do, it tends to be considerably smaller than the increment received by those who publish. This finding holds true for all of the twenty-two fields analyzed in this chapter. Third, those engaged in public service receive statistically significant salary increments more frequently and in higher amounts than those with outstanding teaching skills. Nevertheless, they usually have lower salaries than those who publish. These findings are consistent with the view of the market for labor skills presented in Chapters 3 and 4.

In all fields with the exception of anthropology, those currently engaged in administrative activities receive a large salary increment. In some fields this increment is less than that received by prolific publishers. But administrative activity appears to be an effective way for a faculty member to gain an increase in salary. In fact, because many departments allow faculty members to keep the salary increment they received while they were administrators when they give up their positions, past administrative activity has a statistically significant effect on salaries in most of the fields examined above.

Because the returns to individual skills differ by field, the imposition of a single salary schedule unrelated to field differences will create both equity and efficiency effects of the type discussed earlier. Such effects can be reduced by defining collective bargaining units on a disaggregated basis. But as long as an attempt is made to provide a single salary schedule for all faculty without respect to field, some faculty will be relative gainers while others will be relative losers.

Notes

1. Perhaps the best known of these studies is N. Arnold Tolles and Emanuel Melichar, "Studies of the Structure of Economist's Salaries and Income," *American Economic Review* 58 (December 1968). See also A.G. Holtmann and Alan E. Bayer, "Determinants of Professional Income among Recent Recipients of National Science Doctorates," *Journal of Business* 43 (October 1970).

2. Those with skills that command an equal return to that provided at the common-schedule institution will probably also stay since no incentive exists for them to move.

3. Of course, demand factors also play a role. But the arguments favoring differences by field on the demand side are less compelling than those on the supply side.

4. Some would argue that the true decisionmaker is the dean. Even if this is the case, the extent to which a dean must adhere to the standards of a profession if he (or she) wishes to raise the quality of a department make the arguments in this paragraph equally valid.

5. Distributional constraints could be imposed on universities, such as percentage quotas. But it seems to be a curious approach to public policy to impose incentives that worsen the distribution of faculty on the one hand while attempting to offset the effects of those incentives with yet another policy.

6. An approach that raises the relative return to a skill creates substitution effects in favor of skill development. If skills are not rewarded, the substitution is likely to be toward leisure. On the income side, a policy which raises faculty income irrespective of the skills faculty possess could cause an increase in skill development if skill development is income elastic; it is more likely to cause a

substitution of leisure time if leisure time is more income elastic than time devoted to skill development.

7. Under an economist's definition of efficiency, paying a faculty member an amount more than is needed to keep him or her in an academic position represents a misallocation of resources. However, if the excess amount paid is less than the cost of training a new faculty member, then the single salary approach may still be an efficient one from an economic perspective.

8. An exception to this statement involves the possibility that some faculty will keep up their skills to preserve the option of leaving in the future.

9. Howard Tuckman, James Gapinski, Robert Hagemann, "Faculty Skills and the Reward Structure in Academe," (Forthcoming) *American Economic Review,* June 1977.

10. In many music departments, number of performances serves as a substitute for number of articles in measuring faculty productivity. A faculty member's reputation as a performer also effects his or her salary level. A well-known opera star or composer may enter academe at a high rank and with a high salary, irrespective of his or her publication, teaching, administrative or research skill.

11. It is not clear why past administration is rewarded more highly in English than is current administration.

12. This represents a decrease from the $7,304 earned by law faculty in the 21-50 article category.

13. Because this equation is subject to particularly severe specification bias, we have not reported the regression coefficients here. It seems clear, however, that additional work needs to be done in specifying the determinants of medical faculty salaries.

14. Gerald Otis, John Graham, and Linda Thacher, "Typological Analysis of U.S. Medical Schools," *Journal of Medical Education* 50 (April 1975): 328-38.

15. *Ibid.,* p. 331.

16. Report on Medical School Faculty Salaries, Division of Operational Studies, Association of American Medical Colleges.

17. Howard P. Tuckman and Robert E. Hagemann, "An Analysis of the Reward Structure in Two Disciplines," *Journal of Higher Education* 47 (July/August 1976): 447-464.

18. In biology the median number of articles is 5-10, the category after which salary increments to publication turn positive. The same things happen in the botany equation where the regression coefficients for articles turn positive at the 11-20 article median. In the zoology equation, a positive but nonsignificant regression coefficient is present in the 21-50 median category. These figures suggest that the statistically significant increment to publication in these fields occurs beyond the median number of articles.

The Returns to Publication

Scholarly works frequently are, or at least ought to be, the end product of research. Not that the lack of research activity stops many academics from publishing all the same; but nearly all types of writing produced by academics, with the exception of "creative writing," presuppose some kind of research in the field, the library, or the laboratory.

P. van den Berghe

In this chapter we present a methodology for capturing the direct and indirect lifetime monetary returns to publication. Because the publication skill is the most clearly defined skill of those discussed earlier, and since "publish or perish" issues have been of considerable interest to scholars, we have singled out the returns to publication for individual analysis. The methodology presented here can be applied to the other skills relatively easily, however.

The methodology employed in this chapter is of interest for several reasons. First, it provides a graphic illustration of the fact that decisions made by both the academic marketplace and the academic reward structure have long-term consequences for faculty. Thus, it highlights the future consequences of current decisionmaking. Second, the approach emphasizes the need for information on when in a faculty member's career a skill is acquired. Third, the approach suggests that at least for the publication skill, diminishing returns exist to additional skill investment. This has several consequences for faculty skill development and for the allocation of faculty time which we shall explore in greater detail.

The Returns and Costs of Publication

Ideally, publication provides a means by which faculty share insights, demonstrate creative scholarship, gain recognition for innovative thinking, and establish a reputation for expertise in a speciality area.[1] In some departments, publications are used to discriminate against faculty on the basis of productivity differences; in others, publications are valued because they provide the department with a national reputation. In either case, because publications have value to universities, those who possess them are likely to command a salary premium in the marketplace, other things being equal.[2]

Publication may be rewarded in several ways. First are the direct salary increments that some departments pay for an incremental publication. Evidence of this type of reward was presented in Chapters 4 and 5. The size of these in-crements is likely to depend on the amount available for raises at the time a pub-lication is accepted, departmental (and university) policies regarding merit raises, outside job offers, the quality of the publication, and the tightness of the labor market. Second, in some departments (especially at universities), publication is a prerequisite for promotion to the ranks of associate and full professor.[3] The "publish or perish" phenomenon is well known; less clear is the qualitative im-pact of this type of decision rule. To the extent that an incremental article affects a faculty member's chances for promotion, it has an indirect effect on his salary.

A third type of return exists if a faculty member's career opportunities are affected by the publications he or she has produced. Such opportunities might include outside speaking and consulting engagements, enhanced chances for grant procurement, positions on editorial boards, etc. Likewise, they might in-volve access to internal positions within the university, such as departmental chairmanships and deanships. In either instance, to the extent that publication augments the chances for a faculty member to hold one of these positions, it has a career-option effect.

The nonmonetary rewards to publication are considerable, ranging from self-satisfaction to national recognition. Moreover, evidence exists that effects of this type may be cumulative. An extensive literature has developed, and in-sights into this subject may be found in the work of Merton, Cole, Allison and Stewart, and Marsh and Stafford.[4] Because of the difficulty in quantifying the nonmonetary returns to publication, they are excluded from further considera-tion in this chapter. This does not mean that they constitute an insignificant part of the reward structure, however.

Publication involves costs to the faculty member as well as returns. These costs are usually incurred when a project is conceptualized and researched and when the final results are written up and analyzed. Where publications emerge as the end product of a research project, a reckoning of their costs should probably include the preparation of the grant (or contract) proposal, administra-tive costs, etc. Where publications emerge as a by-product of a faculty member's teaching, the costs should be jointly allocated between the two activities. The same is true for publications that arise as a by-product of public service activity.

The difficulties involved in identifying the costs of publication are fairly serious and deserve extensive study.[5] For present purposes, we have assumed that the full cost of publication is borne by the faculty member's university. This simplification enables us to focus solely on the returns to publication, leaving the problem of allocating costs to future study.

Calculation of the Direct Returns

This section presents the procedures used to calculate the lifetime benefits discussed later in the chapter. Essential to what follows is an understanding of the concept of the marginal or incremental publication. Our goal is to identify the effect that producing one additional article has on a faculty member's lifetime monetary returns. Ignored are the total returns to publication, since we have already examined this question, at least in part, in the last chapter.

The computation is made for all faculty in the twenty-two fields using the regression equation contained in Table 4-1. The choice of this approach, rather than of one estimating separate returns for each field, is based on our desire to examine the average returns to the publication skill for faculty in academe, rather than the returns to a particular field. We have applied the methodology elsewhere to two fields, economics and education.[6]

Ideally, it would be useful to make the computation for both articles and books in order to compare the return to the two. Unfortunately, however, the lack of a well-defined pattern of rewards for book publication suggests that it would be misleading to calculate smooth returns to book publication.

The direct return to an incremental article is calculated in a straightforward fashion. The salary increment to the average faculty member with i articles is subtracted from the salary increment to the average faculty member with $i-1$ articles, after the other factors that cause differences in the salaries of the two groups are netted out.[7] The difference between the two salary increments is then discounted and summed over the average working lifetime of a faculty member to arrive at the direct lifetime returns resulting from the publication of the ith article.

Economists employ a discount procedure to translate a stream of future salary increments into a current equivalent.[8] The theory behind the use of a discount rate is that a salary increment received in the future is worth less than one received today. For example, a dollar put in the bank at a 5% interest rate today may yield $1.05 next year. Thus, it seems reasonable to argue that a dollar received a year from now is worth 95 cents today. Another way to look at present value is to note that it represents the amount a person would be willing to pay to take over an asset with a future stream of income. A bond that promises to pay $50 a year for 30 years and that sells for $950 has been given a present value of $950 by the market. A person who buys this bond places a value on the future stream of income of at least $950.

Present value is a useful concept for examining the academic reward structure because it enables us to analyze the consequences of investing in a skill over the working lifetime of a faculty member. The present value approach tells us what the current worth of publication-related increments to salary might be if a faculty member could sell his or her future salary increments for one lump sum. It also highlights the fact that the lifetime return to an incremental publication depends on the number of years in which the salary increment is received (i.e., at what point in the faculty member's career it was published), the size of the increment, and the rate used to discount the benefits.[9]

Consider the example of two faculty, one an assistant professor and the other a full professor. Assume that both receive a $1,000 salary increment as a result of publishing an article. The assistant professor is age 33 when the first increment is received and 65 when she retires; her increments are received over a 32-year period. The full professor is age 44 at the time of the first increment and 65 at retirement. In this case, increments are received for 21 years. Applying a 5% discount rate from the time the article is published and assuming that the first increment is received in the year following publication, we calculate that the present value of the article is $12,821 for the full professor and $15,803 for the assistant. The difference in the return for the two is the longer time span in which the assistant receives the salary increment.

In reality, the value of a publication may also depend on the point in a faculty member's career when it is written. Given the cross-section nature of the present study and the lack of information on the year in which each publication is produced, we are unable to allow for this possibility. Thus, the regression coefficients from the all-ranks equation are used in making the comparisons of the returns to publication at each rank. This may overstate the return to assistant professors somewhat, but it is preferable to a procedure that focuses solely on the yearly returns to faculty.[10] Should longitudinal data become available for the fields included in this study, the methodology proposed here could readily be extended to allow for differences in the point in a faculty member's career when a publication is produced.

Calculation of the Indirect Returns

Publication increases a faculty member's chances for promotion at many universities. Since promotion normally results in a higher salary, it seems reasonable to include a portion of the salary increase that faculty receive when they are promoted in the calculation of the value of a publication.[11] The problem becomes one of determining the weights to be given to publications in the decision to promote a faculty member to a higher rank. While it is possible to determine the average number of publications for faculty just promoted and the tradeoff between publication and other activities, publication does not, in itself, guarantee promotion to a higher rank. Factors such as congeniality, ideology, and field of specialty enter the process in subtle and often unmeasurable ways.

On the assumption that these factors are distributed randomly across departments, a regression procedure can be used to determine the extent to which publication contributes to promotion. A subsample of faculty consisting of those promoted in the year of and in the year preceding the study is combined with the sample of those not promoted.[12] Separate subsamples are drawn to capture promotion to the associate and full professor ranks. A dummy variable indicating whether each faculty member is promoted is then regressed on that person's publications, administrative activities, teaching and public service, degree level, and experience. The regression coefficients obtained by this process may be taken to indicate the conditional probability that a faculty member with a given number of publications will be promoted, measured net of the effects of other promotion-related activities.[13] The weights obtained by this process are then used to allocate the promotion-related salary increment according to the marginal contribution of each publication to the likelihood of promotion.

Career-related effects of publication are limited to three types: access to department chairmanships, deanships, and other administrative positions at universities.[14] This is because the ACE data do not permit a careful analysis of the nonuniversity-related activities of faculty. Publication may also affect a faculty member's career options in two ways, either directly or through promotion to a higher rank, which increases the likelihood that the faculty member will hold an administrative office. For present purposes, we assume that the sole effect is through promotion. This is done in recognition of the large number of subjective factors that enter into the selection of an academic administrator.[15]

Computation of the Incremental Value of an Article

The publications variables shown in Table 4-1 cannot be used directly to compute the incremental value of an article because of the discontinuities that exist between categories. To approximate a more rational reward structure for publications, the assumption is made that each Table 6-1 regression coefficient represents the salary increment to a faculty member with the midpoint number of publications. A curve is then fit using the function $z_i = AP_i^{-B}$ where z_i is the average salary increment from producing i publications, A and B are constants, and P_i is midpoint number of publications in the ith category.[16] Multiplication of the number of publications by the average value of a publication gives the

Table 6-1
Salary Increments Resulting from Publications

Increment to Article Number	Male		Female	
	Total salary increment	Marginal salary increment	Total salary increment	Marginal salary increment
1	$ 471.65	$471.65	$ 250.14	$250.14
5	1,242.05	156.05	999.45	174.65
10	1,884.70	115.75	1,814.90	157.37
15	2,405.40	97.78	2,572.80	148.28
20	2,860.00	86.95	3,295.60	142.17
25	3,270.75	79.23	3,993.50	137.90

total salary increment received by the average person with *i* publications. Marginal salary increments are obtained by subtracting the total salary increment for a person with *i*—1 publications from the total for a person with *i* articles.

Especially in the intervals where a large number of articles are involved, the use of a midpoint rather than an average or median estimate may understate the value of a publication. This is because the salary increment associated with a given category is divided by a larger number of publications than might be the case if the median or even the average is used.[17] For this and other reasons discussed below, the returns shown in Table 4-1 should be viewed as approximations of the true direct salary increments resulting from publication.

Table 6-1 presents both total and marginal returns for faculty with select numbers of publications. The total column shows the effect of *all* of a faculty member's publications on his or her salary; the marginal column indicates the effect of the particular publication (i.e., the first, fifth, etc.) on the average faculty member's salary. Note that the table shows that the salary increment received for an incremental publication diminishes as the number of publications produced by a faculty member increases. Thus, the salary increment for the first article is substantially greater than that for the second, the second is greater than the third, etc.

Table 6-1 also suggests a pattern similar to that discussed in Chapter 4. The initial increment to salaries from article publication is greater for males than for females. However, diminishing returns set in for males more rapidly than for females, so that by the fifth article, the marginal return to females is greater. Note that the total salary increment to publication for females does not exceed that of males until the fifteenth article.

Several additional refinements might be made in these calculations. It would be interesting to compute the returns to publication net of Federal and state taxes. This would yield a lower incremental return to faculty with a high family income. But reliable data on family size, family income, and the funds from outside employment could not be obtained. Thus, our results are gross of the effects of the tax laws.

It is also possible to allow for salary growth through time, adjust for unemployment and career change, and allow for the probability that a faculty member survives until retirement. Since it is difficult to forecast the future of faculty salaries at this time, and since these adjustments have relatively little effect on the pattern of diminishing returns, we have not made them in this chapter. Thus, the estimates presented above assume that existing salary differentials are maintained through time and that the average faculty member remains employed in academe through retirement.

Direct Lifetime Returns to Publication

In computing direct lifetime returns to publication, two separate approaches can be used. The first assumes that all publications are produced in the same year, while the second allows the time when a publication is produced to vary. For the purposes of the present analysis, we have chosen to employ the former approach for several reasons. As indicated earlier, direct returns are affected by both the value of the salary increment and the time horizon. Thus, it stands to reason that if the twentieth article is published twenty years into a faculty member's career while the first is published after three years, the former is likely to be worth less than the latter. But if both are assumed to be published at the same point in time and diminishing returns are still present, this raises a question about what is happening to cause the market to place a lower value on each succeeding publication.[18] The comparison made below emphasizes that independent of when the ith publication is written, as the number of publications produced increases, the returns per incremental article appear to diminish.

A second reason for adopting the former approach is that the data do not permit us to identify the point in the average faculty member's career when the ith publication is produced. The ACE questionnaire does not contain information on the year in which a publication is written, and given the size of the sample, it is extremely difficult to construct longitudinal career profiles from external sources. Thus, the decision was made to present the lifetime returns by rank and to assume that all publications are produced in the third year following entry into that rank.

The average assistant professor starts in that rank at age 30, the average associate at age 35, and the average full professor at age 41. Under the assumption made above that the incremental publication is produced in the third year and the first salary increment is received in the fourth, an assistant professor receives increments for 32 years, the associate for 27 years, and the full professor for 21 years. No allowance is made for the possibility that a faculty member leaves academe, transfers to an academic job where the publication increment is eliminated, or dies. Likewise, no adjustment is made for the possibility that a publication depreciates in value or that the size of the salary increment depends upon when in a faculty member's career a publication is written. Table 6-2 presents lifetime returns to publication for both females and males.

Perhaps the most interesting finding in this table is the size of the increments that faculty receive from publishing. Note that the lifetime return on the first article ranges from $3,207 for female full professors to $7,453 for a male assistant professor. These amounts are considerable, and they suggest a strong incentive for faculty to engage in at least some publication activity.

The table shows sharply diminishing returns to publication beyond the first article. Note, for example, that male assistant professors have a lifetime return of $7,453 on the first article but only $2,466 on the fifth, a decrease to 33% of the first article. The returns to associate and full professors are

Table 6-2
The Direct Lifetime Returns to Publication

Number of Articles Published	Male			Female		
	Assistant	Associate	Full	Assistant	Associate	Full
5% Discount Rate						
1	$7,453	$6,906	$6,047	$3,953	$3,663	$3,207
5	2,466	2,285	2,001	2,750	2,557	2,239
10	1,829	1,695	1,484	2,487	2,304	2,018
15	1,545	1,432	1,254	2,343	2,171	1,901
20	1,374	1,273	1,115	2,247	2,082	1,823
25	1,252	1,160	1,016	2,179	2,019	1,768
10% Discount Rate						
1	$4,493	$4,357	$4,079	$2,383	$2,311	$2,163
5	1,487	1,441	1,350	1,664	1,613	1,510
10	1,103	1,069	1,001	1,499	1,454	1,361
15	931	903	846	1,413	1,370	1,282
20	828	803	752	1,354	1,313	1,230
25	755	732	685	1,314	1,274	1,193

less on the first article, but they are still sizable. For female faculty, the initial return on an article is less than that for males (i.e., $3,953 for the female assistant professor) but the effects of the less substantial rate of diminishing returns may be observed in the fifth article category, where the return of $2,750 represents an amount 70% as great as that for the first article. For females as well as males, the assistant professor stands to gain the most from publication.

It lies beyond the ken of this chapter to examine whether the returns to article publication are too little or too much. However, it is interesting to note that the presence of diminishing returns may imply that faculty seek out other activities as their number of publications increases. We shall return to this point shortly.

Indirect Lifetime Returns to Publication

Two data subsamples are created, one consisting of assistant professors plus those promoted to associate in the last two years, the other including associate professors plus those promoted to full professor in the past two years.[19] For males, the subsamples consist of 5,094 and 5,665 faculty respectively. For females, the respective figures are 683 and 529. A regression equation is estimated for each of the subsamples in which a person's promotion status is regressed on the individual publication variables, the teaching award and public service variables, a variable for possession of a PhD or other professional degree, and a variable for years of experience. Publication, teaching, and public service

are the traditional factors considered in the promotion process. Possession of a
PhD is included because many universities are reluctant to promote uncreden-
tialed staff. Finally, years of experience is included to control for the fact that
years in rank are often taken into account in the promotion process. The probabilities obtained from the regressions are then smoothed using the same assumption about the midpoint of an interval as discussed above.[20] Table 6-3 shows
the smoothed probabilities calculated for select publication categories.

The figures in this table are read as follows. After controlling for other
factors relating to a faculty member's chances of promotion, a male faculty
member has a 4% chance of being promoted with 1 article, a 9% chance with 5
articles, a 21% chance with 15 articles, etc. What the table shows is that the
probability of promotion rises as a faculty member's publications increase.[21]
The effects of publication are different for males and females. In the full professor regression, at any given article publication level females are more likely
to be promoted than males. The exception is for females with only one published article. In the associate professor equation males are more likely to be
promoted than females in every article category after the fifth.

While Table 6-3 is interesting in its own right, it does not enable us to compute the indirect effects of article publication on salary. The question is "By
how much does an incremental article increase a faculty member's chances for
promotion?" To answer this, the marginal increase in the probability of promotion is used.[22]

A promotion-related salary increment is obtained by multiplying the salary
increment attributable to promotion by the increase in the probability of being
promoted due to publication. For example, the increase in the probability that

Table 6-3
Number of Articles Published and the Probability of Promotion[a]
(In Percent)

	Promotion To			
	Associate Professor		Full Professor	
Articles	Male	Female	Male	Female
1	4.1%	10.2%	0.6%	0.3%
5	9.4	10.2	2.0	4.0
10	15.5	11.3	3.8	9.5
15	21.2	13.4	5.8	11.5
20	26.4	16.7	8.0	13.2
25	31.1	21.1	10.3	14.5

[a]For other things held constant, see text.

a male assistant professor will be promoted to the associate professor rank is 1.1% as a result of publishing five articles. Promotion to associate raises his salary by $1,403. Thus, the promotion-related effect is $15.43 per year, starting at the time of promotion and terminating at retirement. A salary increment due to promotion is obtained by separating faculty by rank and re-estimating the Table 4-1 regressions separately by sex and rank.

The constant term for each of the rank regressions represents the net salary of a faculty member at that rank. A rank-related salary increment is obtained for promotion to the associate professor rank by subtracting the constant term of the associate professor regression from that of the assistant. The same procedure is used to get the salary increment for promotion to the full professor rank. The appropriate salary increments for males are $1,403 (promotion to associate) and $5,459 (promotion to full). For females, the increments are $305 and $6,409 respectively.

The lower increment to female associates appears to relate to the heavy concentration of female faculty in this rank. This is probably a reflection of the vestiges of past discrimination, and it raises a serious question about salary equalization schemes which adjust for discrimination against women by faculty rank along the lines discussed in Chapter 4.[23]

A career-related return to publication is obtained by multiplying the proportion of faculty in a given rank either currently in administration, previously in administration, or on an eleven-month contract by the respective salary increments.[24] The same calculation is made for the next highest rank, and the former figure is subtracted from the latter.

An example is helpful in understanding this process. About 25% of the male full professors in the sample are currently in administration. The average increment they receive is $3,428. In contrast, 10.5% of the associates are in administration, and they receive an average salary increment of $2,345. Thus, promotion to full professor is assumed to result in a career-related salary increment of $490.80 for male faculty. Carrying this calculation out for all three activities yields a career-option increment of $340 for male assistants promoted to associates and of $1,262 for male associates promoted to full professor. The comparable figures for females are $268 and $446. The benefits to females again turn out to be less than those to males.

Indirect lifetime returns are obtained by summing the promotion-related and the career-option returns after these have been multiplied by the marginal probabilities derived from Table 6-3. The resulting figures are then discounted and added to the direct lifetime returns presented earlier in Table 6-2 to derive the total lifetime returns shown in Table 6-4.[25]

Addition of the indirect lifetime returns to the direct returns does not change the basic conclusions drawn earlier. Assistant professors still obtain the largest returns from publication and full professors the least. This is not an unexpected result, since the indirect returns to publication are greatest to assistant professors.

Table 6-4
The Total Lifetime Return from an Incremental Article

Number of Articles Published	Male			Female		
	Assistant	Associate	Full	Assistant	Associate	Full
5% Discount Rate						
1	$8,828	$7,388	$6,047	$5,017	$3,899	$3,207
5	3,034	2,606	2,001	3,253	3,187	2,239
10	2,372	2,016	1,484	2,945	2,855	2,018
15	2,064	1,753	1,254	2,756	2,644	1,901
20	1,931	1,674	1,115	2,554	2,397	1,823
25	1,785	1,561	1,016	2,388	2,177	1,768
10% Discount Rate						
1	$5,220	$4,630	$4,079	$2,957	$2,445	$2,163
5	1,778	1,623	1,350	1,891	1,970	1,510
10	1,378	1,259	1,001	1,707	1,766	1,361
15	1,193	1,085	846	1,603	1,638	1,282
20	1,105	1,030	752	1,499	1,491	1,230
25	1,018	959	685	1,417	1,363	1,193

The returns to each additional publication continue to diminish, even after indirect returns are added. The greatest absolute decline occurs after the first publication. However, the rate of decline is somewhat lower due to the fact that the probability of promotion increases monotonically after the first publication. This is not true for full professors who, given our methodology, gain no indirect returns from publication.

Finally, the returns to publication for females, although somewhat less than those for males in the first category, exceed those of males in every category thereafter.

Implications

Our results suggest that the monetary incentive for faculty to acquire a skill in publication, if only to obtain the substantial returns that accrue to the first article, are substantial.[26] While the present values shown above may not seem large when viewed in an absolute sense, they are fairly large when viewed relative to the returns available from the other skills defined in this study. Of course, what is not known is the additional costs that faculty must incur to obtain these returns. In some fields, this may be significant.

How faculty respond to this incentive is unclear. It is true that some will publish whether they receive a salary increment or not. For these people, peer group recognition, personal satisfaction, or other nonpecuniary rewards are sufficient. It is probably equally true that some will cultivate the skills that offer the highest return for their effort. These faculty will be influenced by how the returns to publication change through time. It is doubtful that faculty calculate the returns to the individual skills in anywhere near the elaborate way we have presented them here. Nevertheless, it seems likely that a differential change in the monetary rewards to alternative skills will become known to faculty and that some will alter their behavior in response.

The results presented above offer a fresh perspective on several issues. Researchers attempting to explain the diminishing rate of publication as faculty age have attributed this to patterns of scientific recognition, the effects of aging, and the nature of the environment.[27] While each of these explanations has some validity, none takes into account the presence of diminishing returns to publication. Because the returns to publication diminish both with age and increased output, additional publications are worth less to older, well-published faculty than to new entrants to the field. The former may find it more rewarding to engage in short-term projects with large rewards such as outside consulting, editorial positions, and contract work, than to continue to publish.[28] This would explain the lower publication rate observed for older faculty.

A similar explanation may hold for the finding that older faculty prefer integrative to basic research. The former tends to be less time-consuming than the latter, leading to a higher return per publication. Of course, the choice among alternative activities is not independent of the cost. An activity conducted on a faculty member's own time may be less attractive than one financed by a grant, given equal returns to both.

It may also be true that as the relative returns to publication shift, the time spent in teaching and public service may shift as well. Thus, decisionmakers unhappy with the current allocation of time in academe may be able to influence it at the margin by changing the reward structure rather than through faculty evaluation forms or mandatory classroom hours. We shall evaluate this possibility further in the last chapter.

Notes

1. In actuality, these goals may not be met. Publications may simply rehash the past, restate existing theories in a slightly different framework, or transmit second-rate ideas. Despite the elaborate mechanisms designed to allow only quality articles to be published, the academic community does not always separate the wheat from the chaff. To its credit, it is still trying.

2. The analysis in this chapter is restricted to universities. But even at these institutions, publication is not always rewarded. See James V. Koch and John F. Chizmar, "The Influence of Teaching and Other Factors upon Absolute Salaries and Salary Increments at Illinois State University," *Journal of Economic Education* 5 (Fall 1974): 27-34.

3. For example, see J.W. Skeels and R.P. Fairbanks, "Publish or Perish: An Analysis of the Mobility of Publishing and Non-Publishing Economists," *Southern Economic Journal* 35 (July 1968): 17-25.

4. Robert K. Merton, "The Matthew Effect in Science," *Science* 159 (January 1968): 58-63; Jonathan Cole, "Patterns of Intellectual Influence in Scientific Research," *Sociology of Education* 43 (Fall 1973): 377-403; Paul D. Allison and John A. Stewart, "Productivity Differences among Scientists: Evidence from Accumulated Advantage" *American Sociological Review* 39 (August 1974): 590-606; John Marsh and Frank P. Stafford, "The Effects of Values on Pecuniary Behavior: The Case of Academicians," *American Sociological Review* 32 (October 1967): 740-54.

5. A simple explanation will suffice. Suppose that as a result of receiving a grant, a faculty member is employed for the summer. During this period, the faculty member engages in research, a portion of which finds its way to an academic journal. Suppose, too, that the faculty member puts in a forty-hour week during the summer. What is the cost of the article? Presumably, if the alternative to the summer grant was no job, the cost could be zero.

6. Howard P. Tuckman and Robert E. Hagemann, "An Analysis of the Reward Structure in Two Disciplines," *Journal of Higher Education* 47 (July/August 1976): 447-464.

7. The reader is cautioned that while regression analysis enables us to capture variations in the salaries of the two groups due to age, sex, region, etc., it does not take factors such as motivation, intellect, and other personality characteristics into account.

8. For a simple discussion of this concept, see Harold Bierman and Seymour Smidt, *The Capital Budgeting Decision*, 2nd ed. (New York: Macmillan, 1966), Chapters 2 and 3. A more theoretical discussion appears in Jack Hirschleifer, *Investment, Interest, and Capital* (New Jersey: Prentice-Hall, 1970), Chapter 2.

9. Economists do not agree on the appropriate discount rate to use. See Jesse Burkhead and Jerry Minor, *Public Expenditure* (New York: Aldine-Atherton, 1971): 228-29. For present purposes, we shall use 5% and 10% discount rates. The reader may choose between them.

10. An alternative procedure would be to use the regression coefficients obtained from regressions separating faculty by rank. See Howard P. Tuckman and Jack Leahey, "What Is an Article Worth," *Journal of Political Economy* 83 (October 1975): 951-68.

11. This procedure assumes that if a faculty member is not promoted, he or she remains at the same rank. To the extent that universities follow an "up or out" rule, the value of promotion is likely to be understated by this procedure. In fact, for some faculty it may be infinite.

12. The sample is restricted to those just promoted, since we felt that the

publications faculty accumulate after promotion should not be counted in determining the appropriate weight publications assume in the promotion process.

13. See Arthur S. Goldberger, *Econometric Theory* (New York: John Wiley, 1964), pp. 110.

14. Data are available on the number of days of outside consulting a faculty member engages in. This is a somewhat weak measure, however, because it is not clear what this variable really measures.

15. Discussions with faculty on a number of campuses suggest that no direct correlation exists between articles produced and the likelihood of becoming a dean or chairman. Thus, the promotion-related approach appears to be the preferred one.

16. The estimating function is $ln\ Z = ln\ A + B\ ln\ P$. *Ln* denotes the natural log, and the variables have already been defined.

17. Thanks are due to John Siegfried for raising this point.

18. For an analysis of the effect of time of publication on the size of the return, see Gordon Tullock, "Universities Should Discriminate against Assistant Professors," *Journal of Political Economy* 81 (September/October 1973): 1256-57.

19. If all assistants plus associates were included in the sample, the regression would capture the effects of a faculty member's current publications rather than of those held at the time of promotion. By restricting our sample to those recently promoted, we have tried to limit this type of bias. It might be argued that first- and second-year assistants and first- to four-year associates should also be eliminated from the samples as not eligible for promotion. The inclusion of the experience variable provides a partial control for eligibility, however, and it seems preferable to an arbitrary set of assumptions about eligibility.

20. A curve is fit regressing the interval probabilities obtained from the regression on the midpoint and midpoint squared of each interval for articles and books. This creates a smoothed set of probabilities.

21. The probability that a faculty member with a large number of articles and books will be promoted is substantially less than 1. This is because factors other than publications enter the promotion decision.

22. The computation can be illustrated as follows. The probability of promotion to associate professor is 16.7% for an assistant with five articles and 15.6% for an assistant with four articles. Thus, the marginal increment to the probability of promotion due to the fifth article is 1.1%.

23. Many female faculty have stagnated in the associate professor rank for years, in part because of the absence of publications (see the marginals for publications in Table 4-1, in part for mobility reasons, and in part because of discrimination. Females now coming through the ranks can probably expect a substantially larger promotion-related increment than the one used here as affirmative action makes its influence felt.

24. The assumption here is that the availability of these positions is a function of the faculty member's rank. It is further assumed that a person entering a higher rank has the same probability of obtaining one of these positions as those already in the rank. As faculty age and the total number of positions in academe shrink, this assumption is likely to become less valid.

25. The discounting begins at the time the publication is assumed to be produced, while the salary increment does not begin until the person is promoted to the higher rank. This procedure renders the direct and indirect returns comparable.

26. Recall, however, that an incentive does not appear to be present in the physical and biological sciences and in medicine and pharmacy. In these fields, the incentives favor those with a large number of publications, and diminishing returns are not present. That faculty publish in large numbers in these fields may say something about the importance of nonpecuniary rewards.

27. For an example of each position, see S. Cole and J.R. Cole, "Scientific Output and Recognition: A Study in the Operation of the Reward Structure in Science," *American Sociological Review* 32 (June 1967): 377-90; H.C. Lehman, *Age and Achievement* (Princeton, N.J.: Princeton University Press, 1953); and J.C. Pelz and F.M. Andrews, *Scientists in Organizations* (New York: John Wiley, 1966).

28. For an interesting analysis of the different publication patterns by field and age using the ACE data, see Alan E. Bayer and Jeffrey Dutton, Career Age and Research-Professional Activities of Academic Scientists: Tests of Alternative Nonlinear Models, paper presented at the American Educational Research Association Meetings, 1975.

7

The Returns to Faculty Skills and the Allocation of Faculty Time

Administrative ability and skill in advertising the enterprise count for rather more than they once did, as qualifications for the work of teaching. This applies especially to those sciences that have most to do with the everyday facts of life, and it is particularly true of schools in the economically single-minded communities.

T. Veblen

The efficiency arguments presented in the last few chapters are based on the assumption that changes in the monetary returns to a particular skill affect the amount of time spent by faculty in both the development and utilization of that skill. While this may be an elementary concept to those trained in economics, it is likely to be met by disbelief by some people. Four major arguments can be advanced against the notion that the allocation of faculty time is sensitive to changes in monetary rewards: 1) faculty are not aware of the monetary rewards to particular skills; 2) the reward structure is constantly changing so that it is difficult, if not impossible, for faculty to adjust their behavior in response to it; 3) the nonpecuniary rewards to faculty are so substantial that they outweigh the monetary rewards; 4) faculty have limited, if any, control over their time.

The argument that faculty are not aware of the monetary rewards to particular skills assumes that the reward structure is not based on a rational set of decisions but rather on the whims of those who hold departmental chairmanships, deanships, or positions on departmental executive committees. While it is true that at particular institutions and particular moments in time, both the salary determination process and the reward structure may be characterized by irrational actions, this argument, if valid, does not rule out the possibility that the process is a rational one when viewed at the national level. The empirical work presented in the last two chapters, as well as the review of the literature in Chapter 2, indicates that a fairly well defined set of variables affect salaries. The evidence also suggests that the markets place values on the skills faculty possess.

It is true that a faculty member deciding whether or not to publish another article may not know if this will add $736, $213, or $100 to his or her salary. As indicated earlier, the exact size of the increment will depend on the amount of merit money available for faculty raises, the number of other publishers in the department, etc. It may also be true that because of this uncertainty, some faculty may be reluctant to invest large amounts in developing their skills. But if the publisher or administrator is consistently rewarded more than the teacher or the person engaged in public service, this may be sufficient to cause faculty to allocate more time to developing those skills that offer high returns. The knowledge that a skill is favored may be sufficient to induce a change in the behavior of faculty members, even if the actual dollar magnitudes involved are not known.

Frequent changes in the reward system may make it difficult for faculty to allocate their time in a rational manner. If research is favored in one year and teaching in the next, faculty will find it difficult to constantly reorient their behavior. As a result, they may choose to acquire the skills that bring the most satisfaction irrespective of their monetary rewards.

The problem with this argument is that it overstates the degree of uncertainty in the reward structure. The emphasis on research in the 1960s created a demand for research skills that lasted close to a decade. While Federal appropriations for research fluctuated during this period (see Chapter 1), the rewards to those who published appear to have been fairly consistent.[1] Similarly, the lack of concern for good teaching suggested in Chapters 4 and 5 appears to have persisted for many years.

The change of a department head, dean, or university president often gives rise to the impression of instability in the reward structure, perhaps because of the resulting shift in emphasis from one activity to another that it may bring. As long as faculty have both the opportunity and the willingness to shift institutions, they can retain the rewards to particular skills when the emphasis shifts, albeit at some cost, by moving.[2] While faculty are not likely to exercise this option frequently, its availability lends greater assurance of a return to investment in a skill than critics of our analysis may acknowledge.

To the extent that the total returns to investment in a skill are derived from two separate processes, one market-related (the salary determination process) and the other institutionally related (the reward structure), the combined return to investment in a skill is likely to be more stable than if the return derived solely from a single source. Thus, for example, publications may be deemphasized in a year of limited salary increases while still receiving emphasis in the decision to promote and/or tenure. In fact, some universities may tighten their publication requirements in a tight labor market in order to increase the output of their junior faculty. Decisions of this type are usually implemented by university committees, as well as deans and department heads. This gives the promotion process a measure of independence from the salary process. A similar independence is observed in the decision to appoint a faculty member to a higher office, an honorary position in an association, etc. Thus, one might expect a greater stability of total returns than would occur if the only rewards to a particular skill came through the salary determination process.

The argument that the nonpecuniary rewards to faculty life are so substantial that they outweigh the monetary rewards will be considered in more detail in the last chapter. It is useful to clarify the argument at this point, however. No doubt, some faculty are unwilling to publish, teach, or engage in public service or administration at any price. But this group is likely to be in the minority. More likely is the possibility that given existing skill differentials, some faculty will not alter their behavior in response to the differentially higher returns to a particular skill. To admit that this is true is not to accept the idea that skill differentials are unimportant or that they have no affect on the allocation of faculty time at the margin.[3] As the monetary differential between the skills increases, the incentive to adjust one's allocation of time to obtain a higher salary also increases. At some point, this may induce a change in faculty behavior. Whether this point is reached at a low return or a high one is a matter of empirical verification.

The final, and perhaps most interesting criticism of the analysis is that faculty have little or no opportunity to control their allocation of time. Those who hold this view take one of several lines of attack. The first is to suggest that as faculty spend time at an institution their time commitments grow, leaving little time for investment in a skill. A variant on this theme suggests that faculty time is controlled by the department chairman or dean. Thus, faculty cannot adjust their behavior in response to changes in monetary rewards. Yet a third variant suggests that faculty begin with roughly equal time commitments but that specialization sets in over time. Those initially successful in exercising a skill become more successful; those who fail to acquire skills initially find less time to develop them (or to maintain them) as they age.[4] As a result, faculty get locked into activities.

Each of these arguments contains an element of truth, and each envisions a constraint on the freedom faculty have to choose among alternative activities. But to argue that any of these leaves faculty with no free time begs the question. Substantial flexibility is available to faculty in choosing the activities they wish to pursue. Indeed, it is precisely this flexibility which attracts some professionals to an academic career. Preparation for teaching can take either a little or a great deal of time depending on the faculty member's inclinations. Time off for research can be generated by successful grant proposals, self-financed summers, fewer leisure hours, or by less time in other university-related activities. While accumulated advantage no doubt has an effect as faculty age, it is by no means certain that this limits the freedom of faculty to trade off their time among alternative uses.[5]

Careful analysis of this issue is precluded by the absence of data both on how faculty allocate their time and on how they wish to. Data on the former are easier to acquire since one deals with what is rather than with what might be. The data sample employed in Chapters 4 and 5 enables us to examine the allocation of faculty time across alternative activities. It is not possible to establish that this allocation is the result of free choice rather than the actions of a department head or dean. The results nonetheless suggest that the time academics spend in alternative activities is a variable rather than a constant.

Wherever possible, we shall also try to relate the findings in this chapter to those in the earlier ones. The reader should bear in mind that the analysis that follows is crude, however, and that a more rigorous exploration of the issues requires both a better data base and a more sophisticated quantitative technique. In the absence of the former, the latter hardly seems warranted.

The Principal Activity of Faculty

One way to examine how faculty behavior changes through time is to look at the principal activity that faculty engage in. Since the data are from a cross-section of faculty at American universities, it is not possible to determine how the principal activity changes for a particular faculty member. The data can be tabulated by experience cohort, however. Subject to the cautions concerning cross-section data outlined in Chapter 3, this provides an interesting insight into how behavior changes as faculty gain in experience. Principal activity is classified into four categories; administrator, teacher, researcher, or other. The classification is chosen by the faculty themselves when they answer the ACE questionnaire. The experience cohorts chosen below are arbitrary ones. Table 7-1 presents the tabulations by sex and experience cohort.

Although the proportion of faculty in a particular activity does not vary in a simple linear fashion with experience level, several useful insights appear to emerge from the table. With one exception, the proportion of male faculty in administration increases with experience. The proportion of faculty who are administrators in the 0-5 year experience level is quite small—6.7%. In the 26-30 experience cohort it is significantly larger—22%. In contrast, the proportion reporting teaching as their principal activity tends to fall, from 81.1% in the 0-5 year cohort to 63.4% in the 26-30 cohort. Given the low returns to teaching relative to administration, this shift is consistent with an economic interpretation of faculty behavior. But one might also have expected a shift out of research.

Table 7-1
Principle Activity of Faculty by Experience Cohort and Sex

Experience	Administrator		Teacher		Researcher		Other	
	Male	Female	Male	Female	Male	Female	Male	Female
0-5	6.7	13.6	81.1	78.0	10.6	3.7	1.6	4.7
6-10	10.8	13.6	74.4	77.0	13.1	5.8	1.7	3.6
11-15	17.3	15.1	65.8	74.7	14.4	7.2	2.6	3.0
16-20	18.7	11.6	67.0	76.1	11.8	9.7	2.6	2.6
21-25	21.5	16.1	67.6	66.4	9.1	11.7	1.8	5.8
26-30	22.0	9.7	63.4	79.0	11.6	4.8	2.9	6.5
31-35	20.5	9.4	66.9	77.4	10.6	9.4	2.0	3.8

The figures do not suggest that this occurs except in the 21-25 year cohort. Since our findings are consistent with other interpretations than the economic one, no conclusions about the importance of monetary rewards can be drawn at this point.

In contrast to males, the proportion of females in administration drops with years of experience; from 13.6% in the 0-5 cohort to 9.7% in the 26-30 cohort. This may be a result of affirmative action policies, which currently offer more opportunities to young females than to older ones.[6] In virtually all of the experience categories except the first two, a smaller proportion of females than of males are administrators.

The proportion of females who are teachers remains the same across cohort groups, except in the 21-25 cohort. In contrast, the proportion in research increases from 3.7% in the 0-5 cohort to 11.7% in the 21-25 cohort; beyond this point the proportion falls off again. Female faculty apparently leave administration to become researchers, a pattern consistent with the high returns female publishers receive. (Recall that the findings in Chapter 4 suggested that the returns to administration are lower for females than for males while the returns to publication, at least for prolific publishers, are higher.) Once again, it is hard to determine whether monetary returns affect faculty behavior. Teaching is unrewarded for females, yet most females remain in this activity. Research is highly rewarded, and some females appear to move into it later in their careers. Thus, the empirical findings appear to be inconclusive.

Common to both sexes is the low proportion of faculty in "other" activities. This finding suggests that few faculty engage in public service as their principal activity and that the three activities discussed above are the most important ones. If part-time faculty were included in the analysis, the proportion in the "other" category would increase.

An Hourly Measure of Time Allocation

An alternative way to examine the allocation of faculty time is to analyze the number of hours devoted to each activity. Although this approach fails to capture intensity of effort, it nonetheless provides a better measure of the amount of effort expended by faculty than does the primary work activity classification discussed above.

Ideally, we should like to cross-classify the average number of hours spent in research, teaching, public service, and administration by field and years of experience. Several data problems prohibit this, however.

The ACE questionnaire utilizes interval rather than discrete categories for the reporting of time spent in alternative activities. Thus, mean hours could not be computed and we were forced to work with the median hours interval in analyzing time spent in an activity for each experience cohort. The problem is that this measure is relatively insensitive to changes in faculty work effort and it gives the impression of discontinuous shifts in the allocation of time as faculty gain in experience. To avoid this difficulty we report the results in terms of the proportion of faculty with less than or the same number of hours as the median in the tables that follow. This measure is less desirable than one that uses the mean number of hours spent in the activity by each cohort but more desirable than one based solely on the median interval. If faculty spend less time teaching as their experience increases, our measure will rise. The opposite is true if faculty spend more time teaching as their experience increases.

It would also be useful to present data for the four activities listed above. Because of the definitional problems and data omissions on the ACE questionnaire, tables are available only for teaching (Table 7-2) and research (Table 7-3). The last row of each table shows the median number of hours currently spent by faculty in that activity. The entries in each cell show the percentage of total faculty with this level of experience spending the median number of hours or less in this activity.

Table 7-2 indicates that for male faculty in virtually all of the fields, the percentage of faculty spending the median amount of time or less preparing for teaching increases somewhat with time. For males in three grouped fields, math-engineering, liberal arts, and the social sciences, the proportion first increases then decreases. For females, the pattern depends on the field. In three fields, the pattern is similar to that for males; biological sciences, liberal arts, and social sciences; in three others, math-engineering, professions, and the physical sciences, time spent in preparation either remains the same or increases. These results further reinforce the impression that females have an affinity for teaching, at least relative to males. Unfortunately, they offer little insight into why this is true.[7]

It is also useful to note the difference in the median hours spent in preparation for teaching by field, since this tends to support the arguments regarding differences in skill intensity presented in Chapter 5. The liberal arts appear to have the largest number of median hours spent in teaching (13-16 for males and 17-20 for females), while the biological sciences and the professions have the smallest, at least for males (5-8).

These differences are considerable, and they imply that the time spent in other activities will also differ widely, an impression confirmed in Table 7-3, where the median hours spent in research varies from 1-4 for females in the professions to 17-20 for males in the biological sciences. Recall that the returns to the individual skills presented in Chapter 5 indicate that publication brings a monetary reward in the biological and physical sciences only when the faculty member has published a number of articles in excess of the median for his or her field. We explained this result by the fact that virtually all of the faculty in these fields had published. The large medians reported here lend credibility to this finding.

Contrasting the median amounts of time spent in research-related activities by males and females, we find that these tend to be the same in three fields; liberal arts, social sciences, and physical sciences. Females spend less time on

Table 7-2
Percentage of Faculty Spending the Median Number of Hours or Less in Preparation for Teaching

Experience	Biological Sciences		Math and Engineering		Liberal Arts		Social Sciences		Professions		Physical Sciences	
	Male	Female	Male	Female	Male	Female	Male	Female	Male	Female	Male	Female
0-5	42.3	a	48.1	58.3	52.2	56.4	54.5	47.8	35.6	68.6	62.0	75.0
6-10	51.5	43.8	58.3	66.8	57.7	75.0	65.7	61.6	54.2	63.7	68.8	70.0
11-15	50.5	59.1	66.8	33.3	79.8	80.8	68.7	64.1	58.0	62.2	68.6	60.0
16-20	54.4	83.2	63.5	50.0	71.1	53.9	70.3	52.5	57.8	56.4	73.1	66.7
21-25	50.9	77.0	59.3	a	65.1	85.6	70.6	53.6	55.2	71.9	69.4	50.0
26-30	55.7	28.6	72.9	a	73.2	63.7	61.8	50.0	68.0	68.0	74.1	50.0
31-35	61.5	71.5	63.0	20.0	72.1	75.1	61.9	75.0	61.6	50.0	76.1	75.0
Median	5-8	9-12	9-12	9-12	13-16	17-20	9-12	9-12	5-8	9-12	9-12	9-12

aDenotes insufficient number of observations.

ACADEMIC REWARD STRUCTURE

Table 7-3
Percentage of Faculty Spending the Median Number of Hours or Less in Research-Related Activities

Experience	Biological Sciences		Math and Engineering		Liberal Arts		Social Sciences		Professions		Physical Sciences	
	Male	Female	Male	Female	Male	Female	Male	Female	Male	Female	Male	Female
0-5	57.3	33.0	49.2	66.6	53.9	64.8	46.4	67.0	62.3	63.4	47.3	20.0
6-10	57.6	44.5	50.1	26.7	49.3	53.7	46.6	60.7	56.1	56.9	42.6	33.3
11-15	63.5	35.0	57.8	66.7	56.0	40.7	55.0	55.5	52.8	52.8	47.8	60.0
16-20	64.9	53.9	58.8	50.0	61.6	77.0	57.0	63.5	55.1	47.4	52.8	a
21-25	74.3	57.1	64.8	40.0	61.8	83.3	57.0	77.7	59.9	51.0	55.8	42.9
26-30	72.0	83.3	54.2	a	50.0	63.7	56.5	66.6	50.0	68.4	62.2	50.0
31-35	74.7	50.0	66.7	66.6	50.7	80.0	57.7	50.0	53.3	50.0	60.5	a
	Median	Median	Median	Median	Median	Median	Median	Median	Median	Median	Median	Median
	17-20	13-16	9-12	5-8	5-8	5-8	9-12	9-12	5-8	1-4	13-16	13-16

aDenotes insufficient number of observations.

research in the three remaining fields. No clear difference between males and females emerges as experience increases. In some fields (i.e., the professions), the amount of time spent in research increases with experience; in most (i.e., math-engineering) it declines significantly. Overall, the table suggests that the proportion of time spent in research, both by males and by females, tends to decrease as their experience increases. This may reflect the possibility that faculty grow more efficient in conducting research as they age, that they make greater use of graduate assistants, that they adjust their behavior to recognize diminishing returns to the research skill, or that they lose interest in research.

The differences in the patterns are worth noting. In the liberal arts, the proportion of faculty spending the median number of hours or less in research first rises then declines for males; in the professions a downward drift takes place for males, but the pattern is ambiguous for females. In the professions, research hours rise for both sexes.

Analysis of the data suggests two points of interest. First, although the correlation is not perfect, in those fields with a high median number of hours spent in research, the increase in the proportion of faculty in the lower end of the hours distribution tends to be larger from the first cohort to the last than it is in fields with a low median. Second, the fields with the largest increases in the proportion of faculty at or below the median are the biological and physical sciences and math-engineering. In most of these fields, knowledge obsolesces quickly.

In analyzing these relationships, it is useful to examine the distribution of research hours by number of articles published. The gross returns shown in Chapter 4 suggest that for the average faculty member the incentive to publish diminishes as the number of articles increases. Thus, hours spent in research might be expected to fall for prolific publishers, ceteris paribus. The accumulated-advantage hypothesis suggests that the costs of publication decrease as the number of articles produced increases. This implies that, other things equal, the number of hours spent in research might increase for well-published faculty. The two hypotheses are compatable only if the costs of publication fall faster than the returns.

Do Prolific Publishers Spend More or Less Time in Research?

To explore the behavior patterns implied by the two hypotheses, the proportion of faculty spending less than or the same number of research hours as the median is cross-classified by field and number of articles. The results are shown in Table 7-4. The reader should be aware that this analysis is necessarily simplistic since it fails to control for the many other variables that affect publication.

Since publications and experience are positively correlated and experience and hours spent in research are negatively correlated (at least in some fields),

Table 7-4
Percentage of Faculty Spending the Median Number of Hours or Less on Research by Number of Articles Published

Articles Published	Biological Sciences		Math and Engineering		Liberal Arts		Social Sciences		Professions		Physical Sciences	
	Male	Female	Male	Female	Male	Female	Male	Female	Male	Female	Male	Female
1-2	82.1	71.4	71.2	74.9	62.0	67.6	62.8	69.7	80.3	69.3	88.0	a
3-4	86.3	90.0	62.5	45.5	60.0	57.6	57.6	71.4	70.1	55.1	81.4	a
5-10	71.1	46.6	55.9	38.5	51.4	52.9	51.5	67.8	61.3	46.9	75.2	70.0
11-20	66.0	26.3	45.2	a	47.8	50.0	45.4	57.1	51.4	42.4	70.4	66.7
21-50	61.2	57.1	44.3	a	34.5	37.5	42.7	46.9	41.8	28.6	66.4	54.6
50+	55.5	33.3	31.5	a	34.9	a	36.6	33.3	28.0	a	58.1	50.0
Median	Median	Median	Median	Median	Median	Median	Median	Median	Median	Median	Median	Median
	17-20	13-16	9-12	5-8	5-8	5-8	9-12	9-12	5-8	1-4	17-20	13-16

aDenotes insufficient number of observations.

one might expect the proportion of faculty at or below the median number of hours of research to *increase* as the number of articles published increases. As is obvious from the table, the opposite relationship exists.

In all fields, and for both sexes, the proportion of faculty spending the median number of hours or less on research decreases as the number of articles published increases. This is particularly significant since the table shows *current* research hours as compared to *past* articles. What it seems to imply is that research effort is less likely to drop off among well-published faculty than it is among nonpublishers or those who publish relatively little. These results are consistent with the accumulated advantage hypothesis. But they alone are unable to rule out the monetary return argument. It remains to be seen whether the costs of an additional publication decline faster than the returns.

It would also be useful to have data on the time input per publication rather than the hours spent on research. These two measures need not be the same since many projects classified as research would not meet the quality standards of the academic journals. Moreover, the time required to write a rigorous theoretical or empirical article is quite likely to be different from that required for a policy statement or philosophical piece.

Research Time and the Allocation of Grants by Discipline

Grants usually free faculty to engage in research. They also reduce the cost of investing in research skills, raising the net return to this form of investment. Thus, it seems reasonable to assume that the way in which grants are distributed affects the allocation of faculty time to research. For example, if a higher proportion of grants is allocated to experienced faculty than to inexperienced faculty, the former group may be more likely to engage in research than the latter, other things being equal.

Data are not available on the total dollar amount of grants held by each experience cohort. Thus, we are unable to determine if these are evenly distributed by experience level. It is possible to identify the total number of grants from Federal, state, local, and private sources going to principal investigators. Subordinate researchers are excluded since we are unable to determine the proportion of their time covered by the grant. Table 7-5 shows the proportion of faculty holding grants in each field by sex and experience cohort. In contrast to the earlier tables, the percentages are read down the columns, and each column sums to 100%.

Table 7-5 shows that over 50% of the grants in most fields are held by faculty with less than fifteen years of experience. In virtually all of the grouped fields and for both sexes, the proportion of grants held by faculty diminishes with years of experience. This is a surprising result, since the accumulated-advantage

Table 7-5
Percentage of Grants Held by Faculty by Experience Level, Field, and Sex

Experience	Biological Sciences		Math and Engineering		Liberal Arts		Social Sciences		Professions		Physical Sciences	
	Male	Female	Male	Female	Male	Female	Male	Female	Male	Female	Male	Female
0-5	10.7	5.7	25.4	30.0	27.5	40.9	28.4	28.2	17.2	15.7	12.8	13.2
6-10	24.3	28.6	30.7	40.0	25.4	29.5	27.2	27.4	21.0	21.9	29.0	28.6
11-15	21.4	14.3	17.7	10.0	16.7	11.4	15.3	15.4	21.0	20.6	19.3	19.6
16-20	15.4	14.3	8.8	a	11.2	2.3	12.3	12.3	15.8	16.9	12.6	12.6
21-25	12.0	20.0	10.0	20.0	9.7	4.5	8.9	8.7	11.6	11.4	13.2	13.4
26-30	7.1	5.7	2.7	a	3.4	4.5	2.8	2.9	7.9	7.8	5.1	5.0
31-35	6.5	8.6	2.1	a	3.4	2.3	3.6	3.7	3.0	3.2	4.8	4.6
35+	2.6	2.8	2.6	a	2.7	4.6	1.5	1.4	2.5	2.5	3.2	3.0

aDenotes insignificant number of observations.

hypothesis would suggest that older faculty enjoy a distinct grant-getting advantage. One might also expect grant givers to place more confidence in those with an established track record.[8]

When Tables 7-5 and 7-3 are compared, an interesting relationship is observed. The decline in research hours corresponds to the decline in research grants. Although not an unexpected finding, this suggests that the pattern of grant giving may be such that faculty with limited experience are ones most likely to receive research support. Once again, a caveat is in order. It may be that young faculty receive small grants to encourage their research while older faculty receive large ones. If so, reliance on the distribution of the number of grants will tend to understate the impact of grants on the time allocation of older faculty and overstate it for younger faculty.

Before leaving this issue, let us briefly return to the accumulated advantage hypothesis. To what extent does a person's previous publications record affect his or her ability to acquire a grant? Table 7-6 shows the proportion of faculty in each field holding a grant. The data are crosstabulated by number of articles published and sex. Although the pattern is not uniform across fields, the results suggest that the likelihood of holding a grant increases for males as the number of articles they have published increases. The pattern for females varies by field with some evidence that the proportion holding grants declines as the number of articles published increases, at least in the liberal arts and professions.

On balance, the results for males offer some support for the accumulated-advantage hypothesis; they are inconclusive for females. This is an interesting finding, for it raises the possibility that the differential reward structure for males and females discussed in Chapter 4 is at least partially the outgrowth of patterns of discrimination that exist in the grant-giving process. Remarkably little research is available on this subject, however, and we prefer to leave it to other researchers to follow up on this possibility.

Summary and Implications

The results presented above show that the allocation of faculty time does not remain constant as faculty gain in experience. While we cannot rule out the possibility that these changes are due to assignments given by employers, it seems reasonable to assume that they at least partially reflect the changing preferences of faculty. For male faculty, there is some evidence that higher-return activities are substituted for lower ones as faculty age. For females the evidence is mixed, supportive for researchers but contradictory for teachers. The ACE data do not enable us to get behind these figures in sufficient detail to explore their implications.

In virtually every comparison, the results are sufficiently cloudy to prohibit a clear test of the hypothesis that faculty adjust their behavior in response to the

Table 7-6
Percentage of Grants Held by Faculty by Number of Articles and Sex

Articles Published	Biological Sciences		Math and Engineering		Liberal Arts		Social Sciences		Professions		Physical Sciences	
	Male	Female	Male	Female	Male	Female	Male	Female	Male	Female	Male	Female
1-2	1.3	11.4	8.2	10.0	16.7	26.8	12.1	15.3	6.7	16.8	2.6	a
3-4	3.9	8.6	14.3	40.0	14.6	26.8	13.9	15.3	8.7	8.8	3.6	a
5-10	14.1	28.6	25.1	10.0	21.4	9.8	22.9	32.0	19.0	18.4	14.5	43.8
11-20	22.8	11.4	21.3	20.0	15.8	2.4	19.8	20.7	19.6	25.6	24.2	18.8
21-50	29.3	25.7	18.1	20.0	15.3	4.9	17.8	6.7	23.7	10.4	31.2	25.0
50+	28.2	11.4	9.5	a	5.0	a	6.9	a	18.1	6.4	23.3	12.5

aDenotes insufficient number of observations.

monetary returns they potentially can receive. Some of the findings suggest behavior consistent with the hypothesis, others behavior that seems contradictory. It is interesting to note that the evidence in support of the accumulated-advantage hypothesis also proved to be inconclusive. These findings may be a function of the cross-section nature of the sample. If so, a final resolution of the question of whether monetary returns affect faculty behavior must await better data. But it is also likely that a more sophisticated methodology is required to separate time allocations based on free choice from those resulting from the constraints placed on faculty time.

Perhaps the most important contribution of this chapter is its finding that the allocation of time to alternative pursuits differs by field. This result supports the argument that different markets for faculty skills may exist by field. But work needs to be done to define faculty skills in greater detail. And it would be useful to develop measures of skill intensity to get at this question more effectively.

Having explored the argument that faculty have little control over their allocation of time, we shall now examine the argument that the nonpecuniary rewards to pursuing a desired activity outweigh the pecuniary ones. This provides a fitting setting in which to conclude the book.

Notes

1. The ACE data are broken down by cohort, and the returns to article publication are then computed for those cohorts in which faculty received their first salary increment attributable to publication during the 1960s. The results indicate a positive and statistically significant salary increment to publication throughout the period. A similar procedure is followed for those receiving recognition as outstanding teachers.

2. Mobility imposes a cost on faculty, if only because of the expense of moving. But the option of moving has a value in its own right, even if it is not exercised.

3. One can envision a range of relative returns over which many faculty will not adjust their behavior as one skill brings a higher monetary reward than another. But if some faculty make the adjustment, the aggregate time distribution will be altered.

4. For the references to this literature, Chapter 6, note 4.

5. What this argument suggests is that since the net return to an activity involves a subtraction of the costs of investing in a skill from the benefits, the return to a more successful faculty member will be greater than the return to a less successful one. This is because the costs are less to the former than to the latter.

6. To the extent that past discrimination has resulted in a deterioration in the skills of older female faculty, it is difficult for them to catch up, if given an equal opportunity with their male counterparts. Some may argue for reverse discrimination to insure salary equality, but this results in salary inequities of the type described in Chapter 4.

7. It is interesting to note that in Table 4-1, 16% of all male faculty and 18% of all female have received an outstanding teaching reward. Evidently, the extra effort expended by females in preparing for teaching is not captured by this variable.

8. This finding differs from that reported by Professor Alice Vandermeullen in her AEA presentation in December 1975. Based on a sample of faculty submitting papers to the *Western Economic Journal*, Professor Vandermeullen found that older faculty are more likely to obtain research grants than younger ones. However, Professor Roland Leibert, using ACE data, found research results similar to mine in his analysis of the determinants of grants. Whether the difference between my study and Vandermeullen's relates to the individual fields covered, the differences in the nature of the sample, or some other uncontrolled factor remains to be seen.

Conclusions and Their Implications for the Reward Structure in Academe

Such is the constitution of the human mind that any kind of knowledge, if it really be such, is its own reward.

Cardinal Newman

The belief that faculty are motivated primarily by the pursuit of the truth, or that they ought to be, is a common one. Thus, it is not surprising that the idea that monetary incentives affect faculty behavior is viewed with disdain by some and with concern or even alarm by others. In the discussion that follows, we analyze the logic behind this point of view in greater detail. Consideration is then given to the relationship between the existing set of constraints and the existing set of incentives and to how this can be improved.

Do Monetary Incentives Matter? The Theoretical Case

It is useful to begin by distinguishing the assertion that faculty are not sensitive to monetary rewards from the belief that they should not be. The former is an objective statement that can be subjected to empirical verification; the latter is a value judgment the validity of which depends on the view of academe held by the person analyzing the question.

Three justifications are usually advanced for the assertion that monetary rewards do not matter: 1) the fact that academics are lower paid than their colleagues elsewhere proves they are not interested in monetary rewards; 2) because success in academe is defined in nonmonetary terms, most faculty are not interested in monetary rewards; and 3) changes in monetary returns are of little consequence for those who have already invested in a skill.

Those who favor the first justification argue that faculty are highly skilled professionals. They often work long hours, exercise considerable creativity, and are dedicated to their work. The salaries these faculty receive are low relative to those obtainable in nonacademic employment; that faculty accept this situation is taken as evidence of a lack of concern for monetary returns. Further support for this view is found in the fact that faculty often undertake work that involves no tangible return, as in the case of journal referees, those on search committees, etc. The presumption is that a person motivated by financial gain would not offer his or her services without a direct monetary reward for the effort. A final

111

piece of evidence, that some faculty continue to work during the summer even if their university does not pay them to do so, puts the finishing touch on the argument.

Unfortunately, the evidence is not as clearcut as might first be supposed. An assistant professor of art might earn more by selling real estate than he does in academe. If he wished to remain an artist, however, it is likely that this person would earn more as an academic than he would by trying to support himself by his art work.

It is not evident that persons willing to specialize in a number of fields represented in academe, ranging from art to English literature, incur a cost by entering academe. It is true that they give up the higher income they could have received in another occupation, and in this sense they show themselves to be concerned less with income than with satisfaction. It is equally true that by choosing academe over self-employment these people may choose a higher income over the satisfaction of engaging in their skill without the interruptions that an academic career implies. Thus, it is hard to infer a disinterest in money from their behavior.

That faculty undertake activities that involve no tangible return is also not self-evident. For example, some journal referees are asked to undertake this activity after their own articles are accepted by the journal. To argue that service as a referee offers no tangible return for these people is to ignore the quid pro quo nature of their contribution to the journal. Similarly, some faculty are willing to referee because this permits them to stay abreast of research developments in their fields before they are published. For these referees, the activity is an intermediate product in the production of research. A similar argument can be made for exchange and criticism of faculty papers.

Even the argument that some faculty choose to support themselves during the summer is not a conclusive one. To the extent that summer work results in book royalties, in the generation of research grants, or in other future monetary returns, it is probably a simplification to assume that this type of behavior provides evidence of a disinterest in monetary rewards. The statement may be true for some faculty but the issue is how large a proportion it applies to.

A second justification for the "money does not matter" view is that success in academe is defined largely in nonmonetary terms; usually by the esteem of one's colleagues, respect for one's knowledge and intellectual abilities, and one's national reputation. The academic with an ostentatious house or an expensive car may gain the respect of his neighbors but little, if any, positive reinforcement from his colleagues. Thus, it seems reasonable to assume that an academic wishing to be successful will eschew activities that are monetarily attractive in favor of those which lead toward greater intellectual recognition.

The propensity of academics to focus on intellectual achievement may be further reinforced if the pursuit of truth brings internal satisfactions at least equal to those available from the acquisition of money. In this case, changes in the monetary returns to a particular skill or set of skills are likely to be ignored,

either because they might divert a faculty member away from the successful
pursuit of a career or because they do not match the internal satisfactions faculty
receive by pursuing their own interests.

Although these arguments describe the sentiments of some faculty, they
tend to oversimplify the real world. Some activities that offer a monetary
return may also be consistent with the pursuit of academic achievement. A
faculty member may obtain a grant that both brings a higher salary and enables
him to obtain national recognition for outstanding work. Likewise, a faculty
member's activities as a paid consultant may result in a contribution to the
existing body of knowledge in her field while increasing her income at the same
time. Money offers at least two advantages to faculty wishing to pursue knowledge:
it buys their free time and it provides the resources needed to gather and analyze
new data.

Of course, not all faculty aspire to the conventional forms of success in
their field. A faculty member with a child of college age, a sick wife, or a desire
to retire on a comfortable income may be willing to trade off nonpecuniary
rewards for more income. This is not to imply that this person will be less
interested in the pursuit of the truth: only that he will allocate his time differently than a person interested in "success" as defined by his profession. Thus,
if an opportunity arises either to spend time doing basic research or receive an
honorarium to address a community group, this person is more likely to choose
the latter.

A third justification for the "money does not matter" view is that changes
in monetary returns are of little consequence for those who already possess a
skill. Some persons argue that skill investment begins in graduate school. For
example, the economist may choose to specialize in theoretical econometrics, the
business school student in personnel, or the lawyer in estate tax law. By the time
they enter academe, those who have completed graduate school may be unwilling
to change their behavior if the returns to particular skills change, because of the
amount of effort they have put into their training. Thus, their behavior is
assumed to be unresponsive to changes in monetary returns.

Other persons believe that the real investment in developing skills useful in
academe occurs after graduate school. Faculty spend time preparing their class
notes, learning survey research techniques, interacting with colleagues at professional meetings, etc. Through time, as their professional careers take shape, some
activities are allowed to languish while others begin to fill a major part of their
day. Skills are developed and the cost of engaging in activities involving these
skills diminishes while the cost of engaging in other activities increases. Thus,
faculty are assumed to be reluctant to undertake activities involving new skills.

A final argument made by advocates of this approach is that as faculty age
it becomes increasingly less profitable from a monetary point of view to learn
new skills. This is because the number of years in which their investment can pay
off decreases with age. As a result, faculty become locked in to a set of skills, and
their response to changes in monetary incentives decreases through time.

In response to these arguments, supporters of the "money matters" approach argue that investment in a skill represents a fixed cost.[1] The real issue is whether the incremental cost of retooling in a skill area is less than or equal to the incremental return from acquiring the new skill. If it is, the fact that a high cost was incurred in investing in the initial skill is irrelevant. If the person wants a higher return he invests in a new skill; if he does not, he keeps his old skill. From this, it follows that as the returns to a particular skill rise relative to the returns to the skills a faculty member already possesses, the incentive for faculty to retool in this skill will increase, other things being equal.

The argument that aging reduces the incentive for faculty to invest in a skill needs clarification. If faculty are oblivious to monetary returns then why should they worry about whether it is less profitable to learn new skills? But if faculty are concerned with monetary returns, this need not rule out a shift of skills. Instead, they may choose quick payoff-low cost skills over short payoff-high cost ones as they age. As indicated in Chapter 6, this may mean more time spent in paid outside consulting, in administration, and in integrative rather than basic research.

Taken in total, the above analysis suggests that a *prima facie* case cannot be made for the argument that monetary incentives are unimportant. While faculty may be less sensitive to monetary rewards than other professionals, at least on average, this does not mean they will fail to respond to a change in monetary incentives. And since at least some activities that result in monetary rewards also augment a faculty member's chances for professional success, it is not obvious that the two need be mutually exclusive.

Having explored the argument that monetary returns do not matter, we shall now consider the argument that they should not matter. Those who advocate this position base their objections on a variety of grounds, each of which involves a value judgment.

Should Faculty Be Motivated by Monetary Incentives?

People who take exception to the argument that faculty are motivated by pecuniary incentives often do so based on the conviction that it is wrong for faculty to be motivated by a desire for monetary gain. Some persons believe that concern with monetary rewards may distract faculty from pursuing the lines of free inquiry, encouraging them to focus on whatever happens to be fashionable with those offering monetary rewards at the moment. Advocates of this view note the flurry of activity over space-related issues in the late fifties, poverty in the mid-sixties, and energy in the early seventies. They also fear that the likely outcome of faculty concern with monetary rewards is the creation of a class of intellectual gadflies whose whimsical flits from topic to topic produce a superficial body of literature in a number of areas and a serious body of knowledge in none.

Of related concern is the possibility that once faculty become beholden to an external financing source their pursuit of knowledge will no longer be unfettered. What distinguishes researchers at a university from those in private industry and government is that the former are free to pursue knowledge in any direction their line of inquiry may lead. The universities play a unique role in providing a climate conducive to this type of research, primarily because they enable faculty to engage in disciplined inquiry with no implied commitments. But if faculty were to become conditioned to the idea that they should engage in scholarly activity for monetary gain, it would only be a matter of time before they would become the captives of external funding sources.

Yet a third argument is made by those who fear that if faculty responded to the existing set of incentives it would be detrimental to students. For example, the existing reward structure offers little, if any, incentive for faculty to improve their teaching. If faculty did respond to monetary incentives they might be even less inclined to engage in teaching than they currently are, assuming that they do not now respond. Similarly, a dim future might await such activities as committee work and curriculum development.

In response to the argument that external funding sources might acquire too much influence over the allocation of faculty time, three points are worth noting. First, it is probably desirable for at least a portion of the faculty at a university to devote time to current societal issues, if only because they bring to bear on public issues a fresh perspective and a healthy respect for the limits on inquiry. The presence of these faculty helps to keep those outside the university honest, and it may well be true that the benefits to society outweigh the costs in terms of faculty time foregone by the university.

Second, while it is true that funding from external sources may take faculty away from teaching and allow administrators less control over the allocation of faculty time at their university, it may also be true that it increases the flexibility of the university. Outside funds may be used to attract more graduate students, increase the capital intensiveness of the teaching program, or hire supplemental faculty.

Third, opportunities currently exist for faculty to use their spare time to earn outside income. To argue that the acceptance of monetary incentives validates the quest for income and reduces the importance of the quest for knowledge is to ignore the fact that such incentives already exist.

The argument that monetary incentives create a class of faculty beholden to their donors is also subject to challenge on empirical grounds. Discussions with a number of Federal personnel responsible for grant management suggest that principle investigators often do not provide research results consistent with the position of their funding agency, even in those special cases when they have contracted to do so.[2] Likewise, it is not clear that if good teaching were recognized with a cash reward faculty would be beholden to students, especially if their teaching efforts were rated by a third party. The danger of outside interference may be more perceived than real, although this remains to be seen.[3]

It is also true that the changing objectives of decisionmakers, be they boards of trustees or regents or Federal agencies, make life uncertain for faculty. But it is hard to argue that this uncertainty leads to a dilution of the stock of knowledge, since to do so requires some knowledge of what types of research would have been done in the absence of the influence of these decisionmakers. It may be that productive faculty would have picked scholarly topics and pursued them in the absence of external funding; it may also be true that less research of any type would have been conducted. Given the lack of a well-defined societal standard for "desirable" research, it is difficult to argue that the directions chosen by outside funding sources were the wrong ones or that recent history illustrates the adverse effects of monetary incentives.

Perhaps the most interesting argument against monetary incentives involves the belief that the allocation of faculty time would be "distorted" if faculty knew what the true system of incentives was. This position has two very interesting implications. First, it suggests that faculty are not aware of the incentives confronting them. We have dealt with this argument in the last chapter. Second, it suggests that the existing system of incentives is defective. It is to this issue that we now turn our attention.

How Is Faculty Behavior Currently Regulated?

Faculty behavior is affected both by a system of constraints and by a system of incentives. The system of constraints consists primarily of the set of often un-related rules and regulations set up to deal with the specific problems with which academic administrators have had to deal. When faculty spent too much time on outside consulting in the sixties, rules were passed limiting the number of days of outside employment; when discrimination against females was finally acknowl-edged, various quota systems were imposed. Rules establish the teaching load of faculty, their qualifications to teach in the graduate program, and a host of other forms of acceptable faculty behavior. In each case, administrative regulations limit faculty behavior, and in each case these decisions were taken without regard to the nature of the academic reward structure and the academic labor markets.

In contrast, the existing system of incentives, both monetary and non-monetary, has emerged from a variety of different sources, including the academic labor markets, the promotion and tenure committees, the journal editors, and the various professional societies. The incentive system differs from the constraint system in two important respects. First, it imposes no mandatory patterns of behavior on faculty. A faculty member can ignore the behavior favored by the incentive system if he or she wishes to do so. In this way, free choice is preserved. Second, it is a more fluid and adaptable system which changes through time. As a result, those forms of rewarded behavior that are no longer desirable are ultimately no longer rewarded. Thus, for example, the rewards to outside consulting diminish as the economy turns downward, the market for new PhDs softens, etc. Likewise, the returns to publication change depending on the size of the average raise received by faculty, the number of articles published, etc.

Observation of the processes at American universities leads one to the conclusion that most management decisions are implemented through the constraint rather than the incentive system. There are several reasons why this is likely to happen. Rules and regulations governing behavior are easy to formulate. They fit nicely into the routine of academic bureaucracy, and because they are explicitly articulated, they are defendable in a court of law. In addition, because they can be written so as to require compliance, they are assumed to be capable of insuring quick alterations in faculty behavior.

In contrast, a system of incentives based either on monetary or non-monetary rewards takes time to design. Its implementation is slow, and its effects on faculty behavior uncertain. Incentives may be difficult to reach a compromise about, and because they are nonbinding on faculty behavior, it is difficult to take a faculty member to task over noncompliance with them.

Incentives do have several distinct advantages, however. They can be used to reward gradations of effort rather than to punish noncompliant behavior. They can also be designed so as to reward an integrated set of behaviors and used in lieu of a set of rules, to encourage time allocations that fit the needs of universities. In addition, they provide more freedom of choice to faculty than administrative regulations, allowing faculty to engage in nondesirable behavior, albeit at a cost in terms of foregone rewards.[4] Where such incentive systems have developed in academe, their existence is more easily explained as an outgrowth of the operation of the academic labor markets and of the informal practices of university committees than of the conscious design of academic decisionmakers.

At least in one sense, the failure of high-level decisionmakers to recognize the importance of these incentives is unfortunate. Faculty behavior is likely to be affected *both* by the set of constraints and by the reward structure, for the reasons discussed earlier. When the two act in harmony, the rational course open to faculty is reasonably clear; when they conflict, it is not clear that faculty will pursue those activities most desired by policy makers. An example will help to illustrate the point; many are available.

Partially in response to public concern over neglect of students by faculty, some state legislatures required faculty to spend twelve hours in the classroom each week. This "twelve-hour law" had several implications for universities. It opened the door to a reduction in the number of faculty, since fewer faculty could now teach the same number of classes. It also sent out a signal to faculty that the legislatures wanted to put a greater emphasis on teaching. However, no

evidence exists to indicate that the reward structure was altered to encourage
good teaching, either at the time of the new rule or thereafter. Thus, the constraint system required faculty to spend more time in the classroom while the
incentive system continued to favor nonteaching activities. A rigorous study of
faculty behavior both prior to and following the implementation of the law
remains to be conducted. There is at present, however, little evidence of an
improvement in teaching, a slack in faculty publication, or an emphasis on new
teaching methods.

A similar situation can be found in the implementation of affirmative action
programs designed to end discrimination against females. Instead of providing
incentives to upgrade the skills of those female faculty who have chosen to allow
their skills to deteriorate or providing rewards to universities that promote females
to positions in which they are underrepresented, the Federal government (and
some Federal and state courts) have proceeded through a coercive system of
constraints. The lack of concern with the incentive system has made it hard for
universities to comply with the Federal mandate. As shown in Chapter 4, current
policies may lead to new inequities for some female faculty and to a worsening
of the ratio of females to males in traditionally male-dominated fields.

Recent efforts designed to deal with the future problems of academe employ
the same myopic approach. For example, many foundations and schools of
education are concerned with the effects of faculty aging on the education students
receive. Noting the limited number of new faculty currently entering academe,
and the large number of tenured faculty with several years to go before retirement,
these persons have advocated a program of early retirements. The problem is
that many versions of such a program are costly, not always desirable for faculty
from either a monetary or a social point of view, and not likely to guarantee that
those faculty who should retire will do so. But early retirement is an easily
understandable concept, and it is simple for the bureaucracy to administer, or
so it seems.[5]

Several alternative approaches based on the incentive system can be used
to deal with this problem. These include exchanges of faculty among institutions,
more sabbaticals, monetary incentives for new curriculum development, increased
use of visiting scholars, and a restructuring of faculty rank hierarchies. These
alternatives are not as tidy, require thought and courage to design and implement,
and, at least superficially, they have a less certain effect than does the early
retirement approach. They may ultimately be cheaper and easier to manage, but
this depends on the particular programs selected for implementation.

The preceding analysis is not introduced to propose that the incentive system
be used to substitute for the constraint system in all circumstances. It cannot.
But the examples presented above illustrate the type of thinking that an awareness
of the importance of the incentive system engenders.

Towards A More Effective System of Rewards

At a minimum, it seems reasonable to argue that academic decisionmakers need to devote greater attention to the existing system of rewards at their university. It is not sufficient to maintain that because decisionmaking is decentralized at the level of the dean or department chairman, the criteria used in the salary determination and promotion and tenure process need not be examined at the university level. The effectiveness of many universitywide decisions, ranging from how many hours faculty should teach to how many students ought to be in a class, is related to the rewards that faculty receive from engaging in an activity.

To legislate on issues that bear on the allocation of faculty time without a clear idea of how the system of monetary rewards affects faculty behavior is bad policy, both from an efficiency point of view and in terms of the likelihood of achieved a desired outcome. Especially in the case of faculty who are skilled professionals, proud of their work, and willing to devote long hours to producing a quality product, mandatory legislation can be counterproductive. At best it alienates, at worst it creates an incentive for evasive behavior.

The reward system can be used to help change the direction of the modern university. Evaluation devices can be developed not only to test the popularity of a faculty member but to measure his or her impact in terms of nationally normed tests, student attitudes, and interest in the subject matter of the course.[6] It may also be possible to test for the retention of knowledge. If teaching were to receive a greater reward, the means to discriminate among faculty might become more refined.

More needs to be done to reward the time faculty spend on PhD dissertations, initiatives designed to upgrade teaching effort, and departmental service beyond the call of duty. That the research in this area is sparse is not only a function of our lack of an educational production function but also a reflection of the fact that faculty salaries bear only a limited relationship to some of the skills faculty possess.[7]

At the same time the importance of research and its handmaiden, publication, should not be ignored. While the best researchers are often not the best teachers, there is little doubt that research experience adds an important perspective to the transmission of knowledge, one that is both more critical and fresher than the perspective faculty have in its absence. This is not to say that every faculty member should be given a light teaching load so that he or she can engage in research. But it does suggest that the system of rewards be set up so that at least some publication is encouraged.

The risk is that the events of the next few years will slow the rate at which society acquires new knowledge. Some would no doubt praise this development, arguing that it offers an opportunity to catch up with the explosion of knowledge in the last few decades. But such a slowdown carries with it the risk of stagnation and the emergence of a reactionary intellectual establishment.

In either event the universities will survive, if only because no other institution is as well suited to the transmission of knowledge from one generation to the next. Society can no more ignore the universities than it can ignore the richness of its cultural heritage or the welfare of generations yet to come. We have explored the nature of the academic reward structure and of its implications in some detail. The evidence is convincing that an academic reward structure exists and that together with the academic labor markets it affects faculty behavior. By their actions in shaping this reward structure in the future, academic decisionmakers will have an important effect on the pace of knowledge and its transmission in the next few decades.

Notes

1. In this context, a fixed cost is one that cannot be changed by the decision of whether or not to engage in further investment.

2. It is equally true that the Federal agencies often contract for research without a clear idea of what they wish their output to be.

3. This statement should not be construed to minimize the danger of outside interference. The danger is there. But steps can be taken to minimize this problem if the designers of incentives wish to do so.

4. Our purpose here is not to articulate a well-developed set of incentives but rather to emphasize that the constraint system may not be effective if it directs behavior opposite to that rewarded by the incentive system. Recall, however, that in Chapter 3 we argued that the reward system was subject to constraints. It would require a separate analysis to develop the relationship between the two in proper detail. Thus, we have not done so here.

5. For an evaluation of this issue, see Hans Jenny, "Early Retirement, A New Issue in Higher Education: The Financial Consequences of Early Retirement," Teachers Insurance and Annuity Association of America, 1974.

6. For example, see Howard P. Tuckman, "Teacher Effectiveness and Student Performance," *The Journal of Economic Education* 7 (Fall 1975): 34-40.

7. This statement does not deny the earlier finding that the market rewards some faculty skills. What it indicates is that a market may not exist for other faculty skills, and in this case, if this type of behavior is desired, new rewards must be created.

Index

About the Author

Howard P. Tuckman has published extensively in the fields of public finance, economics of education, and income distribution. His last two books were *The Economics of the Rich* and *The Demand for Higher Education*. He has published in many academic journals including *The American Economic Review, The Journal of Political Economy,* and *The Quarterly Journal of Economics*. Professor Tuckman has been a consultant to the American Institutes for Research, National Institute of Education, American Association of University Professors, and the U.S. Naval Air Training Command. He has also served as a consultant to several Florida agencies including the Economic Advisory Board to the Governor, the Task Force on Education, the Citizens Advisory Council on Housing and Urban Affairs, the Department of Education, the Department of Administration, and has recently returned from a year as a Brookings Economic Policy Fellow in the Office of the Secretary of Health, Education, and Welfare.